# Praise for *A Place to Belong*

"When you read this book you will be faced with a choice. Will you simply be encouraged by Lisa's example, or will you take action and launch your own Circle of Friends? This book will change the way you think about doing God's work in this world—and you will soon discover that you have engaged in the adventure of a lifetime!"
—Carol Kent, Speaker and Author of *A New Kind of Normal*

"*A Place to Belong* is water for the parched soul. Women long to be loved and accepted, to be able to share the deepest parts of themselves, and to discover that divine purpose that moves them to action. With honesty and understanding, Lisa Troyer will lead you along that life-changing journey."
—Kim Cash Tate, Women of Faith Speaker and Author of *Cherished*

"As a woman who understands pain, guilt, and depression, Lisa bears her soul in this heartwarming guide to finding one's place to belong. She uses the often overlooked women of scripture as references and provides detailed instruction on how the modern-day woman can begin a ministry of healing, affirmation, and camaraderie. Her transparency will motivate the fearful, comfort the regretful, and inspire the hopeful to find relief and significance in her own Circle of Friends!"
—Rachel Lee Carter, Speaker, Professional Model, and Author of *Fashioned by Faith*

"*A Place to Belong* is a REAL book for REAL women with REAL lives. Every page has spoken powerfully to my heart as a woman, a wife, a mom, a friend, a mentor, and a ministry leader. Lisa's book will be one of those cherished reads that I will refer to for the rest of my life. Lisa, thank you for being willing to bring words of healing and encouragement 'for such a time as this.' I KNOW that lives will be touched, changed, and challenged to become the authentic women of God that He calls us to be."
—Kathy Coleman, Founder of Worldwide Mom's Day of Prayer

"*A Place to Belong* is the cry of every woman's heart. In this remarkable book, Lisa Troyer shares her own life experiences, weaves in the stories of others, and then shows you how to belong to your own circle of friends. In this chaotic world, Lisa draws you into a world of spiritual hope where you can learn how to embrace and enjoy the love of God and the love of friends. This is a must-read for everyone."
—Dr. Cynthia Fantasia, Pastor of Service and Women, Grace Chapel, Lexington, Massachusetts

"*A Place to Belong* is a woman's intimate journey with a loving God who refuses to leave her helpless and hopeless. Lisa shares her story of pain and brokenness practically and honestly, along with stories of biblical people who also found God in the midst of their pain. These accounts and the recovery tools she offers can give every woman courage to pursue the Father, who alone can restore hope and bring inner healing."
—Dwight Mason, Lead Pastor, NewPointe Community Church, Dover, Ohio

"Reading *A Place to Belong* is like sitting down for coffee with a close friend, knowing she's going to be completely honest with you. Author Lisa Troyer does an eloquent job affirming the power women have to carry Christ to each other. She calls us as women to use that power, to dare to leave our comfort zones, the havens of false safety we've built for our hearts, and come out into the open— to be our authentic selves as we reach out to one another, real and completely naked, knowing we are totally safe and eternally loved. This is a wonderful book for friends and women's groups to share, using it to encourage our growth as individuals, as friends, and as Christ's followers."
—Ellyn Sanna, Executive Editor of Anamchara Books and Author of *All Shall Be Well*

"It is 1 a.m. and I just read the first chapter of Lisa Troyer's new book, *A Place to Belong,* and I can't wait to read more. I thought a little reading might put me to sleep. . .now I just want to read the entire book. Thanks Lisa, I've got a 6 a.m. flight in the morning. Thanks a lot!
—Mike G. Williams, Comedian, Author, and Missionary

# A PLACE TO BELONG

*Out of Our Comfort Zone
and into God's Adventure*

## LISA TROYER

Foreword by Carol Kent
Author of *A New Kind of Normal*

BARBOUR
PUBLISHING

ISBN 978-1-61626-505-2

Published by Barbour Publishing, Inc., P.O. Box 719, Uhrichsville, Ohio 44683
www.barbourbooks.com

*Our mission is to publish and distribute inspirational products offering exceptional value and biblical encouragement to the masses.*

 Member of the
Evangelical Christian
Publishers Association

Printed in the United States of America.

# DEDICATION

To Bob, my husband, best friend, lover, and encourager.

# ACKNOWLEDGMENTS

Bob, for allowing me to ride along.
What incredible memories! I love you so much.
Jillian and Christian, my Splendid Lady and Little Bebe—
beautiful children, incredible people.
Mom and Dad, for being who you are. I couldn't be "me" without you.
LeeAnne, the "eye" of the heart we wish to share—
what a gift you are to COF.
Linda, for exposing me to the "music of the soul."
Beth, as we keep Our Father laughing.
Dawn, trusted interpreter of my "dreams."
Jocelyn, messenger of truth.
Missy, the gentle voice of reassurance.
Brenda and Sharon, protector of the treasure, my resources, my heart.
Missy G., the artist who brings beauty.
Tammy and Tanya, my Throne Dwellers.
Your dedication to intercede is incredible.
Dayna, our GPS. How you have helped me!
Jennifer, for the refuge of rest and comfort.
Teresa and Faith, for healing hands and hearts. Physician and
counselor extraordinaire.
Walnut Hills Prayer Warriors, grandparenting the circle.
Peg, Dee Ann, and Libby, for love and cough drops.
Carol Kent, for loving God, women's ministry, and me.
Carolyn Meininger, for sharing Dan with me and the world. The Word
proclaimed and hearts transformed.
Susan Martins Miller, for drawing me out and writing it down.
And to all who have blessed me and Circle of Friends Ministries—
this is only the beginning.

# CONTENTS

## ACCOUNTABILITY
We encourage you to receive the comfort of companionship. Bet set free!

## ACTION
We pray you will step into your journey. Walk in your purpose.

## RESOURCES FOR YOUR CIRCLE OF FRIENDS

# FOREWORD

## by Carol Kent

The ring of the phone pierced the silence and awakened me in the middle of the night. My husband picked up the receiver, and I saw shock and horror in his eyes. His words stunned me as he spoke with overwhelming emotion. "Jason has just been arrested for the murder of his wife's first husband." Our only child, a U.S. Naval Academy graduate, had fearfully obsessed over the multiple allegations of abuse by his wife's first husband, and it appeared this man was about to receive unsupervised visitation with his two vulnerable little girls. Our son did the unthinkable—and a man died. Our lives turned upside down.

I experienced deep fear—both for my son and for the family of the deceased. My husband and I made our living through my speaking ministry, and we had no idea if we would be able to continue to survive emotionally or financially. We needed a safe place where we could talk with someone about what had happened, where we could process our own fragile emotions, and where we could find spiritual encouragement and know that we would be accepted and not judged by those who knew our story. You may have read about our journey in *When I Lay My Isaac Down* (NavPress) or more recently in *Between a Rock and a Grace Place* (Zondervan).

Over the next few weeks and months, God brought people into our lives who became the hands and feet of Jesus to us. They called themselves our "Stretcher Bearers," and they ministered to us in tangible ways through helping to meet our emotional and financial needs—but most of all, they provided a safe place for us to be vulnerable about what was going on in our minds and hearts. They listened without judgment, and they made us know that no matter what choices our son had made, we were loved and accepted—no strings attached. They encouraged us to continue to minister to others through retreat and conference ministry and to be vulnerable and "real" as we honestly shared our story with others. They covered us with prayer.

On one of those ministry weekends I got better acquainted with Lisa Troyer and her remarkable Circle of Friends. It didn't take long for me to realize our relationship would result in much more than a weekend event—it would be an enduring friendship. Lisa's passion for God, love for people, compassion for those in need, and her intentional encouragement to the women in her life got my attention. One of the things I had been hearing repeatedly from women all over the country is that I was so blessed to have "a safe place" to share our unthinkable circumstances, and that they had great fears about whether they would be accepted if the women around them knew their secrets.

As I observed Lisa's ministry, I realized she shared truthfully about her struggle with depression, and she had created an atmosphere where other women felt comfortable being honest about their own struggles. More than that, I saw a woman who used her leadership, influence, and resources to open doors of opportunity for other women to develop their spiritual gifts, grow in their knowledge of God's Word, and find their significance through their identity in Jesus Christ.

Instead of drawing attention to herself, Lisa has the discernment to discover the giftedness of the women around her, and she creates platforms on which they can use their abilities to make a positive difference in the lives of others. Lisa has created a "Circle of Friends" that can be duplicated all over the country as women learn the concepts of (1) acceptance, (2) authenticity, (3) affirmation, (4) accountability, and (5) action. The principles you will learn in this book will give you the ability to develop a biblical, transformational, and encouraging ministry to the women within your own sphere of influence.

One of the things I like best about the Circle of Friends is that you don't have to be perfect to belong to the group. You can "come as you are," with a lack of faith, a history of wrong choices, and a huge list of questions about life and faith, and you will be welcomed. I think God smiles as Lisa uses her gift of encouragement as a radio host, a lyricist and recording artist, a writer, and a speaker for his kingdom glory.

When you read this book, you will be faced with a choice. Will you simply be encouraged by Lisa's example, or will you take action and launch your own "Circle of Friends"? This book will change the way you think about doing God's work in this world—and you will soon discover that you have engaged in the adventure of a lifetime!

Carol Kent,
Speaker and Author
*Between a Rock and a Grace Place* (Zondervan)

# Beautiful

Who doesn't want the attention
Captured by what captures them
His beauty and grace like a sonnet I can't write or say
Accepted for who in You I really am

When I look at myself through Your eyes, I'm beautiful
When I feel Your hand holding mine, I am Yours
When You reach into my life, You take the wrong and make it right
I'm beautiful 'cause You're beautiful to me

Who hasn't dreamed of redemption
Who doesn't long to be free
Just as I hope for a love that never turns away
You give me all my heart will ever need

When I look at myself through Your eyes, I'm beautiful
When I feel Your hand holding mine, I am Yours
When You reach into my life, You take the wrong and make it right
You wrap my shame up in Your love for me

I'm beautiful, You're beautiful
I'm beautiful because I see the work You've done in me

When I look at myself through Your eyes, I'm beautiful
When I feel Your hand holding mine, I am Yours
When You reach into my life, You take the wrong and make it right
I'm beautiful 'cause You're beautiful to me

—Lisa Troyer/Alan Farris/Tom Michael
© 2010 House of Napoleon Publishing/
BMI/ZodLounge Music/ASCAP

When I was working on an album called "Meet Me at the Well," something tugged at me. We had a collection of inspiring songs, but somehow the album was incomplete. On an October afternoon in Nashville, I told the producer we were not quite finished. "I want every woman to know she is beautiful," I said.

The song "Beautiful" resulted from that wrestling. I first sang it at Grace Chapel in Massachusetts. Afterward a woman in her sixties said to me, "I've been waiting to hear that song my whole life."

In her sixties. No woman should have to wait that long to know she is beautiful to God. If I look at myself the way the world tells me I look, there's always something else I'm supposed to be. But if I look at myself from the perspective of what Jesus has given me—the way God looks at me—I'm beautiful.

I want you to know you are beautiful. That's what this book is about.

# ACCEPTANCE

We welcome you to embark on an adventure in relationship.
Come as you are.

# 1

# I Had a Secret

*This is my story. Acceptance means you can tell yours.*

Day after day for four years in high school, I felt his eyes on me. His aftershave lingered in the aisle as he walked past rows of students, and I remember what his presence felt like when he stood close to me.

I kept his secret all that time and for many years afterward. Protecting him was not my agenda. I thought I was protecting myself.

I was not going to be one of *those* girls.

I was not going to get that kind of reputation.

He was a married man, and I was not going to give in to what he asked of me.

School is supposed to be safe, for crying out loud. He had no business doing the things he did, and I knew that at the time. But I was fourteen, a freshman in high school, and I didn't want to walk the halls in my small-town high school and have everybody see the cloud of inappropriateness that hovered over me. Who would whisper behind my back? Who would pull away from me if they knew?

So I kept quiet.

He asked me out, and I kept quiet. He made physical passes at me, and I kept quiet. He offered to purchase alcohol for a friend, and I, sadly, accepted the offer. I remember the warm spring day in early May of my sophomore year when he asked if I needed anything for the weekend and suggested he join me for a drink. And I kept quiet. He looked at me in *that* way, and I kept quiet. I felt ashamed and confused, and knew this was wrong, but I kept quiet. I sat in his classes every year and earned awards. He was part of my day, part of my routine existence, and no one but my best friend ever suspected the things he suggested to me in private moments. She did not know everything, but she knew something was going on. But she kept quiet, too.

I wasn't the first girl with whom this teacher behaved in inappropriate ways, and I wouldn't be the last. I knew just enough about his previous victims to know their reputations were trashed. He was the predator, but they paid the price, and I was not going to let that happen to me.

So I said nothing.

But I had chronic stomachaches, repeated severe colds, wanted to sleep all the time, and hated going to school. School was never my favorite activity to begin with. I preferred to read what I was interested in and found little wonder in things that didn't apply to my focus du jour. The heightened emotional pressure in high school made attendance even less motivating. My junior and senior years were especially difficult. My interest in music was increasing, but so were my level of frustration and signs of clinical depression, though I didn't know the phrase at the time. I wonder now how I didn't flunk out of school. Two elements of relief were my choral and humanities classes. I enjoyed singing and reading *Wuthering Heights* and other classic literature. I was thankful for the positive influence and encouragement of Penny McKey and Connie Evans, true educators in every sense of the word. Despite my emotional challenges, I managed to make the honor roll and progress toward graduation.

When I was a senior in high school, my stomach trouble took the form of a duodenal ulcer. Because the symptoms persisted after the ulcer healed, the gastroenterologist suggested my parents explore a psychological reason for my illness. I started seeing a psychologist, who officially diagnosed my clinical depression. His practice was not faith-based, but he had studied for the priesthood before getting married, and he encouraged my own faith. It was a safe place for me to say I was not okay without saying *why* I was not okay.

I still kept the secret.

After a while, my father had his doubts that the psychologist was doing any good, but I had recently turned eighteen. By the grace of God, the psychologist reminded me I no longer needed my parents' permission to see him, and he offered to treat me for free for a few months. We spent a lot of time talking about my poor dating choices and areas of my life where I felt I had little control. Looking back now, I realize the therapist probably suspected more than he ever expressed. He was waiting for me to be ready to talk.

But still I said nothing.

My free visits with the psychologist got me through the months until graduation, and then I was free from that environment. I never had to see that teacher again. I was off to the Art Institute of Atlanta, far away from my small Midwestern town, to prepare for a career on the business side of the music industry.

## You can't just walk away.

Just because I did not reveal what happened during high school did not mean the experience had no effect on me. It was years before I told anyone the whole sordid truth and faced the huge impact it had. The depression that began during those years has been a specter for all of my adult life.

On the outside, things looked good. My dad wanted me to take his financial investment in my education seriously, so he said, "No bad grades and no partying, or the money stops." I didn't intend to give him a reason to cut me off. I now enjoyed school. I was free from my tormentor. I could be anybody I wanted to be. People who struggle with depression and don't take prescribed medications tend to medicate themselves with something else, and that's what I did. I plunged into a whole new social life where no one had even heard of my school or the predator who gave me an ulcer. I amassed a new cadre of friends and relished the freedom of living in an apartment by myself. I even dated a young man who presumed we would marry someday—although I knew I would never marry him. Social activities stimulated me and became the core around which my life revolved. I looked forward—never back. I was grown up now, I thought. The past was behind me. I was never going to live in my hometown again, so I had no reason to dwell on the things that happened there. After graduation from the exhaustive one-year program and an internship with the retail division of Zondervan, a publisher with a music arm, I was ready to take on the world.

In those days, a career in the music business meant New York, Los Angeles, or Nashville. My parents objected to Los Angeles, and I had no desire to move to New York. That left Nashville. So off I went with a classmate. We planned to share expenses. Neither of us had a job, nor any prospects, but the hope of youth springs eternal. However, my friend soon found that Nashville was not the place for her and resumed her vocation of ministry and education. So I was on my own.

And I still carried my secret.

In Nashville, at the ripe old age of twenty, I found a niche on Music Row, a historic area that is home to hundreds of enterprises involved in country, gospel, and Christian music. Record labels, publishing houses, recording studios, video production companies—they're all there. I found a job singing demos for a studio in a music publishing company, but ultimately I wanted to work for a Christian company.

I kept inquiring at Benson Records, a major Christian music publishing company that belonged to Zondervan at the time. I grew up in a family business, and I knew the easiest department to get into was sales, where the turnover is always high. So I just kept asking. Eventually I got a job. The woman who hired me said it was not because I had any experience that impressed her. Rather, my tenacity captured her attention. So I jumped into the sales department ready to give it everything I had. Six weeks later, a job in the copyright administration department opened, and she recommended me for that promotion since I'd had some experience on Music Row with similar tasks.

My stubbornness paid off, and I had what I wanted. I was independent. I was out of the Midwest countryside. I was on my way to a career on the business side of the music industry. I worked for a Christian company.

I stayed in Nashville long enough to know I didn't want to work for someone else the rest of my life. The family dairy business that was the backdrop of my childhood had imprinted me with a different mind-set. I had proven I could bulldog my way into the music scene in Nashville, but for what? My parents ran their own business and employed dozens of other people. In addition to his solid business, my dad was always pursuing interests he loved. He even bought a plane. I understand my father. He is never one to shy away from a challenge or an adventure. I wanted to find that elusive intersection between work that paid the bills and being involved with activities that brought meaning to my life. When Dad invited me to return home and join the family business, I took him up on it. I could have the security of the business behind me while also exploring what kind of ministry God had planned for me.

When I chose to move back to my hometown, people thought I had lost my marbles. Didn't I realize how hard it was to get a job at one of the country's largest Christian music companies? If I walked away now, I might never get another chance.

My broken past was behind me. At least, I convinced myself this was true. I was twenty-four years old—a lifetime away from that high school girl with a secret—and embarking on independent music industry consulting. I worked for Cliff Richard, one of England's most popular recording artists, from a base in the rural Midwest. I also jumped right into making cold calls to find new distribution outlets for specialty items of the family business and turned out to be pretty good at the job.

But I still had a secret.

## SECRETS MAKE YOU LONELY.

Secrets can destroy from the inside. When I kept my secret, I thought I was protecting myself, but instead I isolated myself from people who cared about me. I put up a wall to try to keep myself safe, but instead I kept out people who would have wanted to help. I regret all the years I didn't tell my mother what happened. As a teenager, I wanted to avoid the attention that surely would come from exposing the predator—my mother would have made sure he lost his job. He continued to prey on high school girls and eventually was found out. I just didn't want to be the one who made that happen, and I was clueless about how deeply the events would affect me as I launched into adulthood. As hard as I tried to pretend that what happened didn't matter after I left high school, the episodes haunted me for years.

All these years later, I still feel naked telling this story, even without including the details. But I hope we are going to travel together on the road to a transforming life in God, so you need to know that this happened to me. In the pages ahead, you'll read about a lot of heartache. Some of it is mine, some of it reflects the lives of women I know, and some of it rises from the pages of the Bible. And yes, there are some sordid details God thinks we need to know!

Keeping a secret doesn't make it go away.

Putting on your mask doesn't change what's in your heart.

As well hidden as your secret is, that's how deeply lonely you will be. I've been there. I know it's true.

So I tell you my secret and invite you into my journey with God to encourage you to step into your own journey with God. I'm not suggesting you publish your innermost wrestling in the daily newspaper or on a blog or a billboard. But I do hope you will begin to see the bountiful blessing that can come to your life if you unclench your fists and let go of whatever you have been hiding from yourself. From others. From God.

Circle of Friends is a ministry of women who both seek and offer a place to belong, a place of acceptance, a place of truth and love.

This is my story. Acceptance means you can tell yours.

# 2

# THE GOD WHO SEES

*Acceptance means being willing to receive from God.*

After several years away, it was nice to be home for a while. I worked in the family business, got involved in church music, and worked for Cliff Richard. I did not know where any of it would lead, but I was there to find out.

One fall day, my cousin Kim called and invited me to a football game. She and her husband, Larry, planned to ride a charter bus to go see the Cleveland Browns play. Larry was bringing a friend named Bob, and they wanted me to come along. It was sure to be a fun outing, so she did not have to twist my arm too hard to make me say yes. However, I pictured sitting on the bus chatting with Kim while the guys hung out together. Instead, Kim plunked down beside Larry and left me to fend for myself with Bob during the bus ride.

I'd met Bob when I was much younger. We'd even been out together once. Although he was pleasant and nice looking, in those days, living in our hometown was not on my agenda. My desire for city life quelled whatever attraction I felt. Now things were different. We were both older with a better sense of the kind of people we did not want to date anymore. This time Bob and I hit it off from the start. Love blossomed, and the endorphins flowed generously. Although the old depression lurked under the surface, for the most part I felt well and functioned productively. Bob and I shared a lot of interests, had fun, and felt comfortable together. It didn't take us long to decide to marry.

We would be married for years before the changes began.

Bob figured out that if I started working ridiculous hours, something was wrong. But he didn't know what to do. I remembered that the antidepressants I took during high school made me feel like a zombie, and I was not going to do that again. At the time, I had no idea that several new medications were available. I thought I just had to press through on my own.

But it wasn't working. I knew it, and Bob knew it.

Finally, Bob said, "Do you think you should see somebody?"

"What am I going to say?" I responded. "There's nothing wrong."

I had a husband who loved me, and I enjoyed my work. We were healthy. Our families were nearby and enriched our lives. What was there to complain about? I couldn't point to anything that needed fixing. So I didn't see a mental health professional.

Yet some days my strongest urge was to sit and cry. I knew God wanted something better for me, but I still sat and cried. It was as if I were abandoned in a wilderness with no idea what to do next.

## JOIN HAGAR IN A MOMENT OF GRACE.

When I read Hagar's story in the Bible, I can identify—not because we went through identical circumstances, but because we had an identical need for comfort from God in a wilderness.

Hagar's story appears in Genesis 16. She was an Egyptian maid in the household of Abram and Sarai, more commonly known as Abraham and Sarah. Most likely they acquired her services during the time they spent in Egypt because of a famine (Genesis 12:10–20). Egypt always seemed to be the place that had food in times of famine. It would appear that Hagar was minding her own business, working as Sarah's maid, when Sarah came up with a scheme that involved her.

Abraham and Sarah had no children—no small shame in those days. Sarah was past childbearing years, and Abraham was even older at the time God promised Abraham that his descendants would be as innumerable as the stars (Genesis 12:1–9). How in the world was that going to happen? Years went by. No son. Abraham was a decade older, and if he died without a son, his estate would go to his top servant—who might not feel any obligation to care for Abraham's widow. So perhaps Sarah figured it was in her best interest to make sure Abraham had a son somehow, even if it meant bringing another woman into the marriage. She offered her maid, Hagar, to Abraham, encouraging them to sleep together. She suggested she could have children through Hagar. At least such a child, such an heir, would be her husband's true son.

As a maid in the culture of that time, Hagar perhaps did not have a lot of choice in the matter. Abraham apparently agreed with Sarah that it might be time to take matters into their own hands, regardless of what God had promised so long ago. So he slept with Hagar, and Hagar got pregnant. The plan worked perfectly!

Enter emotions. Now Hagar had something to hold over Sarah's head. She was having the baby Sarah tried for decades to conceive, and she didn't miss an opportunity to rub it in Sarah's face. The balance of power shifted, and Sarah was not happy about it.

In the modern world of surrogate pregnancies, we hear in the news every now and then about a woman who withdraws from the agreement after she's pregnant. She wants to keep the baby she agreed to bear for another woman. Things get ugly emotionally and legally. The triangle that developed between Abraham, Sarah, and Hagar was similar. Hagar had something Sarah wanted, and it gave her a sense of power. This, in turn, deepened Sarah's despair. The

> One of the most difficult things for any person is to find a place of genuine acceptance. The tendency is to work at doing whatever it takes to feel as if you are accepted. With Circle of Friends, that is not the case. Acceptance seems to come automatically as soon as you are introduced to the group. A sense of true camaraderie enveloped me from the beginning. Does this mean my behavior is always accepted? No. My circle of friends lovingly confronts anything detrimental to my health—spiritual, physical, or any other form. Because I know so firmly that they accept me unconditionally and are willing to journey through life with me, needed changes in my behavior come more easily. —Libby

baby wasn't even born yet, and already the two women were circling around each other, each determined to be the winner. When Sarah came up with her plan, she did not anticipate this turn of events. In trying to solve one problem, she made a bigger mess.

Now Sarah told Abraham, "It's all your fault! Do something!" Her own choices had backed her into a corner, and the only way out was to blame someone else. How many of us still try that? Abraham tried not to make things any worse than they already were and told his wife, "Look, she is your servant, so deal with her as you see fit" (Genesis 16:6). That's all Sarah needed to hear to make the maid's life miserable. Hagar decided she'd had enough. Baby or no baby, she just couldn't tolerate living with Abraham and Sarah for another minute. Abused and brokenhearted, she fled into the wilderness on her way back to her homeland.

The angel of the Lord found Hagar beside a desert spring, an isolated moment of hope in a wilderness journey. This is the first time the Bible mentions the angel of the Lord. Notice that the angel of the Lord knew who Hagar was and got right to the point. He asked, "Hagar, Sarai's servant, where have you come from, and where are you going?" (Genesis 16:8). To Hagar, this man likely appeared to be a stranger she met at the well, but when he called her by name, the scenario changed. He knew exactly who she was and where she came from. I can just hear Hagar stammering around for an explanation before confessing that she was running away. And then the angel told her to go back to her mistress—and submit to Sarah's authority. This was not an easy pill for Hagar to swallow.

Now the angel spoke in the first person—"*I* will give you more descendants" (Genesis 16:10 emphasis added)—and it became clear that God himself had met this woman in the wilderness.

Hagar chose to run away, and God sent her back. God did not promise Hagar's suffering would end. Sarah might still be cruel, and God's words suggest Hagar's son wouldn't have an easy life. But God did make plain that he would be present with Hagar. "The LORD has heard your cry of distress," the angel said (Genesis 16:11). Hagar would have a son, and her son would have many descendants, which was an enormous blessing in the culture. Even the child's name would remind his mother of her encounter with God. God declared the boy's name would be Ishmael, which means "God has heard."

God noticed Hagar. God met Hagar in the wilderness at her most desperate moment. When she thought her only option was to run away from her troubles, God reminded her of his presence in her suffering. Hagar's eyes were now fully opened. She realized that this was not just a man looking for water in a desert well. She called her visitor "The God who sees me." God cared enough about her to reveal himself in her darkest experience, and Hagar responded by affirming that she knew God was with her.

God saw Hagar. God saw me in the years of keeping a secret. He saw me in my depression. And he sees *you.*

How much we all want to be seen—to feel that someone notices—and cares!

## GOD SEES YOU. AND THAT'S GOOD.

At various times in my life, I knew God was speaking to me and essentially asking the same questions he asked Hagar: What are you doing? Where are you going? We can be overwhelmed by grief, disappointment, and pain. No matter how we do the math, it adds up to zero. Escaping the circumstances seems to be the best option, even if we don't know what lies ahead.

I want to make clear that I am not advocating that anyone should remain in a physically, emotionally, or sexually abusive relationship. If you find yourself in one of these situations, please seek help through your pastor, a counselor, a trusted friend, or other community resources. But for many of us, the real issue is that we are weary of the load we bear and perhaps have come to the point of feeling that we have no good options to make things better. Like Hagar, we just want to leave it all behind. Remember that God sees you. No matter your pain, God sees you and is there. In the days when I wanted to sit around and cry for no apparent reason, God saw me. The journey may be dark, but God is in it with you.

Hagar ran toward Egypt. This was her home, and she assumed it would be a place of refuge. We do the same thing.

*If I could just find the right church, people would finally understand me.*

*If I could just meet the right man, my life would turn around.*

*If I could just get out of my difficult marriage, I would be happy.*

*If I could just find a job worthy of my skills, I would get the respect I deserve.*

*If I could just find that one thing, make that one choice, it would make everything better! Then I wouldn't be alone. I would matter to somebody.*

Don't let Satan deceive you. God does see you. He knows your misery and is present with you when you feel beyond despair. God, the lover of your soul, passionately asks you to walk with him. Flesh-inspired quick fixes to the problems of your life are a dime a dozen—and they don't work. You won't find a diamond in the Cracker Jack box. Sarah thought she had it all figured out, and her plan backfired. Hagar tried to play her trump card—Abraham's heir—and ended up feeling as if she couldn't go on. I've earned a PhD from In My Own Strength University. It doesn't work.

Jesus said, "Are you tired? Worn out? Burned out on religion? Come to me. Get away with me and you'll recover your life. I'll show you how to take a real rest. Walk with me and work with me—watch how I do it. Learn the unforced rhythms of grace. I won't lay anything heavy or ill-fitting on you. Keep company with me and you'll learn to live freely and lightly" (Matthew 11:28–30 MSG).

Hagar encountered God at a well on the road to Shur, and she had to choose her next step. Should she continue to Egypt in the vague hope the refuge she dreamed of would be there, or should she return to Sarah's household in the certainty that God saw her? Recognizing that God saw her—and cared—did not solve all of Hagar's problems. But she stepped into the journey with God and returned to Sarah.

Finding a place to belong—where people notice you and care—begins with accepting that *God* notices you and cares. He sees you. He hears you. He knows your misery. You don't have to go it alone. God is there.

It's not an easy lesson. I won't pretend that it is. But I invite you to consider what God has for you that you might miss if you press on thinking that you can figure things out on your own and don't need anybody else. Acceptance means being willing to receive from God, the One who sees.

# 3
# AT THE WELL

*Acceptance means moving through what holds you back.*

If theology were music, I would be in a jazz band. You get into the groove and you swing! I played saxophone in high school, and my sister Linda is an accomplished jazz musician with several recordings to her credit. Because of her influence, I used to listen to vintage recordings of jazz greats—Charlie Parker, Billy Cobham, Dave Grusin, to name a few.

The thing that always fascinates me about this musical genre is that it can seem rhythmically chaotic, yet have real flow, purpose, and destination. Some of the patterns are unbelievably detailed, yet they flow in a manner hard to describe in words. It's something best understood by experience. The listener is never quite sure where the melody is going to go next, but if you let yourself trust the "master's touch," as it were, jazz evokes a soothing, exciting confidence that it's all good! You *feel* jazz.

If a mere human can take a piece of metal and passionately direct the ebb and flow of a composition, how much more confident can we be in our trust of "the God who sees"? The rhythms of our lives may seem as chaotic as a jazz melody, but when God is singing the tune, we can be sure it will be a good one.

But we have to let go of something. If you go into a jazz performance expecting to hear a Mozart piano concerto, the experience will never measure up. It's not going to be Beethoven or Schubert, either. It's not going to be the Beatles or Garth Brooks or any other popular artist of our own time who doesn't play jazz. When you listen to jazz, you'll enjoy it most if you don't expect it to be something else. Let go of those ideas of music and let yourself experience jazz.

Stepping into a journey with God is like that. We often go in with expectations. This is a list of what God is like. This is how to "do" the Christian life. This is the proper way to pray. This is how God will speak. This is how to show faith. When our spirituality doesn't happen that way, we think we must be doing it wrong.

The notes that make up music are what they are. They don't change, but the composer arranges them in a unique fashion for a specific piece of music. Some songs are similar in melody, to be sure, but each is unique. God doesn't take one of his children's songs and say it belongs to another child. He's so incredibly creative that he writes a unique melody for each of us with the same absolute truth that he himself does not change.

No two people have an identical experience with God. The spiritual life can wander around like a jazz melody, finding its home base once in a while only to jump off again in another variation on another instrument. God is the same God, but we need to find ways to let ourselves experience him freely, rather than trying to fit him into a predictable pattern. We need to discover the beauty of those "unforced rhythms of grace."

## JESUS MEETS US AT THE WELL.

Hagar met God unexpectedly at the well on the road to Shur and discovered him as "the God who sees." Because of that encounter, Hagar found the strength to go back to the responsibilities of her life even though things were far from perfect. Centuries later, another woman went to another well, ashamed of her life, and she met Jesus there. If one passage in the Bible has been a marker passage to change my perspective about who I am and who God is, it's the story in John 4 of the Samaritan woman who goes to the well in the middle of the day. This story of deliverance and forgiveness—of life transformation—is at the heart of God's call for me to encourage other women in honest relationships with God and each other.

Let's start with the skinny on Samaria, the region where this story takes place. It involves a brief history lesson. God promised land to his people, and he delivered on his promise. The Hebrews enjoyed military victories and conquered the Promised Land. But over the generations, the people didn't do such a great job of sticking with God—or each other. The kingdom split into two parts that squabbled with each other. Eventually the northern kingdom fell to the Assyrians, who carted off a good portion of the population into captivity. Foreigners came in to resettle the land and secure the territory for Assyria. These foreigners intermarried with the Jews left in the region, and over the years their descendants were known as the *Samaritans*.

By the time of Jesus, the Assyrians were long gone and the Romans were in charge. But Jews of pure descent still had their noses in the air about the Samaritans, whom they considered half-breeds. Although both Jews and Samaritans traced their common ancestry back to the days of Jacob, they couldn't get along with each other. And the practical problem was that the region of Samaria was smack in between the Jewish areas of Judea to the south and Galilee to the north. Generally Jews traveling between Judea and Galilee would opt to go close to twenty miles out of their way to avoid traveling through the heart of Samaria. In the days of walking everywhere, that was a lot of miles! That's how much the two groups despised each other.

But Jesus felt differently.

John tells us that Jesus left Judea to go to Galilee, and he walked right through Samaria. He stopped in the middle of the day at Sychar, a Samaritan village that was also the location of Jacob's well, a site with historical importance to both Jews and Samaritans. His disciples went off to buy some food, leaving Jesus alone for a divine appointment.

Jesus knew where he was supposed to be. His choice to travel through Samaria arose from his obedience to his Father. Whether it was the politically correct thing to do was beside the point. Jesus had the Holy Spirit without measure, and he knew where he was supposed to be—and when and why.

We also see Jesus' humanity in this story. John tells us Jesus was tired. He was weary from the long walk during the hottest part of the day, hungry enough to send his disciples off in search of food, and thirsty enough to ask a strange woman—a Samaritan, no less—for a drink of water from the deep well of Jacob. Jesus took the physical cue to rest and restore his body, and this opened the door for a moment of ministry. I can't help wondering what moments with God we miss when we ignore our physical needs for rest and restoration. That's an area of my life that my Circle of Friends is quick to remind me to consider.

Most women in the village would come to the well earlier or later in the day, not at noon when the sun was fierce. As we soon discover, something about this woman's life made it easy to understand why she would rather endure the heat than the wagging tongues of the hags from town. She had nothing to lose by engaging in conversation with a Jewish man who ought to know better than to talk to a Samaritan woman. Well aware of the prejudice between the Jews and Samaritans, she was curious why this man would treat her differently. "Why are you asking me for a drink?" she asked, not shy in the least.

Jesus cut right to the chase and took the conversation to the next level. "If you only knew the gift God has for you and who you are speaking to, you would ask me, and I would give you living water" (John 4:10).

The woman didn't quite make the leap and focused on the impossibility of what Jesus said. He didn't have a rope or a bucket, and the well was deep, so how would he get any water? Besides, what kind of nonsense was this *living water*? This was Jacob's well, after all. Was this stranger saying he was better than Jacob?

Jesus was there for a purpose and stayed on the topic. If the woman wanted to know the difference between the well water and living water, he'd tell her. "Anyone who drinks this water will soon become thirsty again," he said. "But those who drink the water I give will never be thirsty again. It becomes a fresh, bubbling spring within them, giving them eternal life" (John 4:13–14).

Ah, now he had her attention. She knews the significance of a promise of eternal life, and she wanted this gift. Where this water would come from was unclear, though. Her mind rushed to how wonderful it would be not to have to come to Jacob's well ever again. Her days of avoiding the village gossips would be over.

Once again Jesus raised the level of conversation. "Go and get your husband" (John 4:16).

"I don't have a husband," she answered. Technically this was true, but she didn't fool Jesus.

"You're right!" he said. "You don't have a husband—for you have had five husbands, and you aren't even married to the man you're living with now" (John 4:18).

Can you see her jaw drop? She thought she was having a clever conversation, a rare moment of social contact, and now a complete stranger was telling her life story.

"You must be a prophet," she said (John 4:19)—and then turned the conversation away from her personal life to the division between Jews and Samaritans. She was an intelligent woman who seemed to be accustomed to maneuvering around men. Her defense mechanisms were fully functional. This was likely not the first time she skillfully distracted a conversation away from herself during an awkward moment. Yet she also seemed genuinely interested, and after Jesus talks about true worship, she put herself back into the conversation. "I know the Messiah is coming" (4:25). She was waiting for the rescue that she knew God planned.

And then came the moment of revelation that this rejected, defensive woman did not expect.

"I Am the Messiah!" Jesus said (John 4:26).

This announcement inspired the woman to action. She forgot all about her water jug. She forgot about her shame. She forgot her reasons for coming to the well at an off hour. John tells us that she went back to the village and said, "Come and see a man who told me everything I ever did!" (John 4:29).

Her past was still her past, and she had no reason to think the villagers would have changed their opinion about her during the brief time she was away fetching water. But her encounter with Jesus—with truth—freed her from her shame. It was okay that she hadn't been perfect. Her mistakes didn't separate her from Jesus. This woman understood that God could take those mistakes and transform her. She had a new purpose.

## Acceptance wells up into hope.

This nameless woman's story gives me incredible hope. The secrets of my past do not determine who I am in God's eyes. The God who sees knows all about those things and meets me at the well anyway. My imperfections do not mean that God does not accept me or that he does not want to reach out to me. Jesus went out of his way to meet the Samaritan woman in this ordinary moment of her life and changed her forever.

A woman who lived shrouded in half-truths and detached from real relationships now had a different view. She wanted everyone to come and meet Jesus. The Samaritan people, along with the Jews, waited for the Messiah but did not know how the promise would come. Once this woman knew the truth—the Messiah was right there—she wanted everyone to know. She understood that the village people with their proper lives and social standards were waiting for transformation just the way she was.

> I was concerned about being accepted because of my divorces, but the ladies with Circle of Friends not only drew me in but also embraced me as I drew closer to them. I have a hard time with guilt, but they love me despite my sordid past. They realize that is not who I am today. They lovingly accept me as their sister in Christ. They did not know me before, but they know me now. —Jennie

Even the people we think have it all together need Jesus. We see the outside of other people's lives, the public perceptions they want us to see, and draw conclusions that everything is hunky-dory. But the truth is, everyone has secrets and mistakes and regrets and wounds that need healing. The church is no different. We get so used to the way we do things that when we see someone come along with fresh enthusiasm about God moving in her life, or in the life of a church, it's easy to be snobby and pretentious. We forget how deep our need was when Jesus first came and sought us out.

Perhaps the most startling element of this story is how the villagers responded to the woman's announcement. She took a chance and stopped protecting herself. Instead, she told her story honestly and freely to the people whose lives intersected hers, and they responded. John tells us, "Many Samaritans from the village believed in Jesus because the woman had said, 'He told me everything I ever did!' " (John 4:39).

When Jesus' disciples arrived with some food, he said to them, "My nourishment comes from doing the will of God, who sent me, and from finishing his work" (John 4:34). That verse has stayed with me for years. In fact, these are the words that first plunged me into the story of the Samaritan woman at the well. Jesus had a purpose. His purpose came from God. Doing what God asked him to do nourished Jesus. Because he did what he was supposed to be doing, the woman's life was transformed and she found her place in relationship and ministry with the people around her.

We need the reminder of people like this Samaritan woman to challenge us to see the things in our own lives that keep us isolated. We need to be women who go to the well seeking to have our spiritual thirst quenched. We need to be women who ask the hard questions and face the blunt realities. Our shame cannot hold us back from encountering Jesus and being part of God's good news.

Don't let shame keep you from Jesus. Don't let cultural issues keep you from asking the deep questions. Don't settle for a life of isolation and avoiding other people who might challenge you. Jesus is at the well waiting for you. Come as you are.

# 4

# HAPPILY EVER AFTER—NOT

*Acceptance means knowing you're not alone.*

Bob and I decided to have a baby. We were both thrilled when we learned I was pregnant. And the doubly wild blessing was that my sister Lee-Anne discovered she was pregnant around the same time. Our due dates were a month apart, so of course we fantasized about how wonderful it would be for our children to grow up together being best friends.

And then I miscarried.

First trimester miscarriages may be fairly common, but statistics are no comfort when it happens to you. At a local department store, I found a T-shirt with images of Bugs Bunny's pursuer, the Tasmanian Devil, all over it. On really bad days after my loss, I wore that shirt. Perhaps it was a humorous or even bizarre way of expressing my mood, but it was strangely therapeutic. I picked myself up and went back to work, even traveling for the family company. Many nights I would stay in my hotel room and cry, mourning the child I would never bear. I dreamed of hearing a baby crying and looking for the baby, only to find it no longer alive when I reached it. When you miscarry, you never really get closure. Most of the time, you don't know why it happened, and you just want to take back the moment when it did.

Months passed as I quietly mourned. A year after the loss, an employee was giving me a hard time at work. He was being insubordinate toward me and causing dissension in my relationship with my now former brother-in-law, who also worked in the business. One day everything erupted. I argued with my brother-in-law about this employee, and before I knew what was happening, my ears were ringing and my vision tunneled. I started to cry and couldn't stop. Pent up for a year, my grief now poured out in uncontrollable wailing. My brother-in-law was rattled and clueless about what to do.

"I want Quinn," I finally said. Quinn was my sister's son who was the same age as the child I would never hold in my arms. "I want to hold Quinn."

My sister and brother-in-law lived next door to the business, so he raced home to get his son. With the baby in my arms a few minutes later, I wept and wept. Exhausted, I still held Quinn, who lay in my arms quiet and beautiful and perfect. Even though he was not my baby, somehow holding him was a comfort. Quinn and I enjoy a sweet relationship to this day. Even though he's now well over six feet tall, I still call him "Pugsley," and he doesn't seem to mind.

When Bob finally got me home from that emotionally exhausting day, I slept for eighteen hours straight, and then I took a week off of work. There's no telling what was going through the minds of the people who witnessed my breakdown a full year after my loss. That was the least of my worries. I was coming apart at the seams and didn't know what to do about it.

During that week I made a decision. I was a mess, and I had too much baggage to think I could ever straighten myself out. And I wasn't sure I ever wanted to have another baby.

"You're better off without me," I told Bob. "This is more than you signed on for. You shouldn't have to live your life with a mess that doesn't know how to be different. It would be better for both of us if you just go find somebody else."

I meant it. I was a wreck. Why should my husband sacrifice his happiness to stay married to me when I didn't know how to be anything but a wreck? He was a loving husband, and he would make a great father and a wonderful family man, but staying with me would cause his life to be much harder than he deserved.

"You should leave me," I repeated.

Bob's eyes met mine. "That is never going to happen."

He took care of me and waited for the cloud to lift. Several days after my meltdown, we went out to dinner to a nice restaurant, but I couldn't sit still. I couldn't just sit there with people milling around and wait for food and pretend everything was normal. It wasn't normal. I didn't even know what normal was anymore. But if I stayed in that restaurant, I was going to lose my grip again.

"We need to go home," I told Bob. And so we did.

The cloud of depression was dense and dark, and I couldn't just think cheerful thoughts and make things better. It doesn't work that way. I felt bad for my parents, always wondering, *Is she better now?* And Bob was giving far more than he was getting out of our marriage at that point. I just wanted to be alone during the most challenging times. But gradually, almost imperceptibly, I got better. Never wanting people to tiptoe around me, I tried not to let my internal imbalance be obvious. One small step at a time, I pushed myself until I was functioning at a level that could pass for normal in the eyes of an onlooker.

## DRAW STRENGTH FROM EXAMPLES.

I wasn't alone. Bob never wavered even a fraction of an inch in his commitment to me. Both our families extended unconditional love and support toward me.

Mothers-in-law are the brunt of so many jokes that I sometimes wonder if there can really be that many inept women in the world. After all, these are the women who brought up the men we choose to marry. I loved my mother-in-law. Raised in a conservative Amish environment, Mary was the oldest of eight children. I remember the first time I met Bob's parents. Mary was the most unassuming person I'd ever met, and I felt comfortable with her immediately. Their home was nothing fancy, but I was always welcome. Mary and Mose decided to leave the Amish lifestyle, and Mary became a women's ministry leader in the community. Her leadership was genuine servanthood bathed in prayer. She touched the lives of more women than I can count, but she would stand at the kitchen counter and talk to me. I knew

I mattered to her, and I felt like I could be myself. I understand why Ruth, in the Bible, wanted to stay with her mother-in-law, Naomi, even when it meant moving to a new land. Mary Troyer was light-years away from the eye-rolling derogatory remarks so many people make about their mothers-in-law.

Mary was a woman who knew grief and loss. When my husband was ten, his young adult brother was killed instantly in a freak accident. Mary knew the pain of losing a child. She also had chronic back problems because of scoliosis, faced cancer, and suffered with Parkinson's disease. Late in life, the cloud I knew so well settled on her, too. After one Sunday dinner, Mary asked to talk to me. We sat on the bed together and she said, "I think you understand how I feel. I don't think anyone else does. I feel depressed. Will you just hold me?"

What a gift! I held her, knowing that sharing that moment with her reminded both of us we were not alone. She saw me. She knew what I suffered over the years. Time and again she had been the one to sustain me in fervent prayer and encouragement, and now I could do the same for her.

Another strong figure in my life is my mom, Nancy Dauwalder. Our family lived right next door to the family business. My mom kept the books for the company, but she always was home for my sisters and me. I had a stay-at-home-working mom. She didn't stand on privilege because she was one of the owners. If a female employee had a sick child, Mom always said, "Stay home. I don't want you here while your child is sick." She never docked her pay either.

My mother was very protective. If she had known what was happening to me in high school, she would have waged an all-out campaign to have the predator removed. I didn't want the attention at the time, so I didn't tell her, but I never doubted what she would have done for me. Years later, after she knew the truth, my mom ran into the man in the elevator of a local professional building. She told me, "I looked at him, and he knew that I knew. His eyes hit the floor, and he could not get out of that elevator fast enough."

## Draw strength from the circle.

You don't need to be alone. That lesson took years to unfold in my life. Instead of protecting me, secrets isolated me. Pretending I was happy when I wasn't did no one any good, least of all me. Left untreated, my depression and anxiety attacks affected a wider circle of people than I imagined. Family, friends, and coworkers stood by, ready to care about me. It took me years to realize, and genuinely believe, that I had people in my life who would stand by me no matter how ugly things got—if I would just let them. And the truly beautiful part of letting other people in was the realization that I had something to give back.

That's the heart of Circle of Friends. We need each other. Acceptance means knowing you're not alone. My mother-in-law modeled ministry to women in the way she walked through her own days, in addition to the events in which she was involved. My mother responded with care to the realities of women's lives. Both of them showed me how strong and purposeful women can be in the ways they connect with each other.

But being strong does not mean you don't feel pain in your life. Being purposeful does not mean every moment feels successful. I want you to know that you do not have to present an invincible front to the world. You don't have to hold things together so that no one sees what you are really like. You don't have to wait until you have a panic attack at work or in a public setting before you understand that being connected to other people—other women—will enrich your life. Your own circle of friends, wherever you are,

*Within the Circle of Friends I have been offered undeniable love accompanied by life-changing truth. I have experienced embracing arms and unconditional acceptance. I have had the opportunity to more fully understand the mercy and grace of God and have grown closer to the Lord surrounded in heart and spirit by women who love him wholeheartedly and encourage me in my faith. They offer to journey alongside me with authentic, transparent, and vulnerable hearts. I have found a family of women I cannot imagine not being a part of for the rest of my life. —Tanya*

can come around you in a time of need. And with acceptance, you can rally around the friend who feels she is stretched too thin or that what she holds inside herself is too fragile for public display.

You can try to cope alone. We all try at some point. But I'm here to say there is no virtue in getting along without feeling safe and accepted anywhere in your life. It doesn't make you holier. It doesn't make you a better Christian. It's not what God calls you to do.

The Lord is "the God who sees." He sees *you*. Jesus waits at the well for *you*. You can't hide behind shame or secrets or the notion that you should somehow be able to manage on your own. Even when you feel most alone, God is there. You can find him in the faces of people close to you, and you can reflect his presence to thirsty souls God puts in your path.

# 5

# FINDING SIGNIFICANCE

*Acceptance means recognizing your need to belong.*

I live in the heart of Amish country. Literally half of the county's population is Amish. Talk about craft central! All around me every day are examples of craft expertise and supreme domestic skills.

And I'm not good at any of it. That's just not me.

In my youth, women's ministries were potluck dinners and sewing circles. To fit into a women's group meant being ultra-domestic and developing a certain set of practical skills. While my mother made sure she was available to her children, she was still a significant player in the family business. I grew up against a business backdrop more than a domestic one, and I have dealt with a lot of men in business environments. I find cooking therapeutic at times, especially around the holidays. Enjoying a great meal together or trying a gourmet coffee is a great way to invite someone to belong. But in general, I'm not going to pretend to be some sort of domestic diva.

That doesn't mean I'm not interested in women's ministries. This book grows out of my passion for a relational style of ministry between women. Meeting Jesus at the well releases each of us to do what God calls us to do. God has a purpose for me, and God has a purpose for you. Together we can discover the joy of living lives that fulfill his purpose.

## WOMEN OF SIGNIFICANCE COME FROM STRANGE PLACES.

When I talk about women's ministries—women ministering to and with each other—one of my favorite parts of the Bible is the first chapter of the New Testament. Matthew begins his account of the life of Jesus with a genealogy that goes back to the time of Abraham. It's easy to skip over "so-and-so was the father of so-and-so." We might figure that the real beginning of Matthew's literary effort is when he starts to talk about Mary and Joseph and how the birth of Jesus came about. But there's some good stuff in that genealogy. Matthew takes care to mention a number of women among Jesus' ancestors.

Matthew begins the genealogy with Abraham, and because we know so much about Sarah's journey in faith alongside Abraham, I can't help thinking about her. God promised them a son, and that's where the lineage that led to Jesus started. Abraham's son, Isaac, fulfilled God's promise for a son, and the generations of descendants leading to Jesus—and beyond—fulfilled the promise of descendants as innumerable as the stars.

But what about the other women in this genealogy? Matthew seems to go out of his way to mention some memorable women among Jesus' descendants.

Tamar, who was neglected by her family and used her own resourcefulness to get what she had coming.

Rahab, a prostitute who was not even from the Hebrew people.

Ruth, an outsider from Moab who loved her mother-in-law and found the true God along the way.

Bathsheba, who was taken advantage of and remembered for being caught in a web of sin.

Mary, young and innocent and unknown, who became the mother of Jesus.

What I love about this list is how clearly God makes room for women to be significant in his plan to redeem the world. Beginning with Abraham and ending with Jesus, in Matthew's list we see God at work in human history to carry out his purpose. Obviously all the men in the list had mothers, but culturally, fathers and sons mattered far more than mothers and daughters. Matthew could have written a genealogy that did not pause to identify any women at all, and his first-century readers would not have noticed anything missing.

But he takes care to mention these women by name, and centuries later their names evoke their stories in our minds. We're going to look more closely at women in Matthew's genealogy as we journey together through the pages of this book. Their struggles for relationships and lives of meaning are not so different from ours. But for now I want you to ponder the truth that God used a string of unlikely women in his plan. This was a culture where women barely rated as more valuable than the furniture—and sometimes less than the livestock. God plucked women out of the shadowy beige landscape of their lives and plopped them down in the middle of the vibrant, colorful story he was rolling out for all of humankind. God was present in their lives, and he is present in your life.

You matter. You matter to God, and you matter to other people.

I've been involved with women's ministries for more than a decade. I've had the privilege of participating in large conferences of women as well as small group conversations. God graced me with the opportunity to host a program on the Moody Broadcasting Network as a way to reach women, and I sometimes hear directly from my listeners. The ministry of Circle of Friends also has a daily conversation with women over the radio. I've had my own issues with believing that I matter, and I hear the same theme over and over from other women.

*Do family and friends even notice everything I do for them?*
*Are mistakes going to haunt me for the rest of my life?*
*If I tell the truth, will anyone love me?*
*In the grand scene of things, does my life amount to anything?*
*How can I think about ministry when I'm lucky to get a shower?*

## You aren't the only one.

Everybody has issues. But so many people feel as if they are the only ones.

The only one with a husband who seems not to see you.

The only one at church with a rebellious teenager.

The only one who can't quit smoking.

The only one whose baby hasn't slept through the night in four years.

The only one who hides a bottle of wine in the clothes hamper.

The only one with a promiscuous past.

The only one whose Uncle Charley cornered you in the basement.

The only one who had an abortion and hasn't been the same since.

The only one whose sister hasn't spoken to you in seven years.

The only one whose father left your mother for a male life partner.

*One of my favorite things as I lead Bible studies on behalf of Circle of Friends is watching women who didn't know each other previously leave the study as close friends. Women who didn't know each other's struggles now help to carry the burden as they pray for one another. They collect phone numbers around the table so they can get together later for coffee. A circle of friends is a safe place to be real, to learn from each other, to laugh together and love each other well. God meant for us to travel through life together. I prayed for women to walk with, and he has gifted me with some of my closest friends. —Jocelyn*

I could keep going, but I think you see the point. You are not the only one. You really aren't. While you're lonely and think that no one can understand what you're going through, other women are just as lonely as they travel their own roads. Circumstances may not be identical, but emotional realities are strikingly similar.

Imagine what life could be like if you told just one person your deepest ache. Imagine what it would feel like to talk freely with just one person about your faith questions and puzzling decisions and life dreams. What if you had three or four people like that? How would that transform how you feel about your life?

We need each other to reflect on the road behind us and ponder what lies ahead. As companions on the journey, we help each other see God's truth rather than our own fears.

Can you believe that God sees you and accepts you just as you are?

Can you believe someone else could know the truth and not reject you?

Can you believe that you could hear another woman's truth and love her anyway?

The journey begins with relationships of acceptance, and those relationships of acceptance are rooted in God's love for each one of us. Because we are valuable to him, we are valuable to one another, and no one has to be alone. We belong to God, and we belong to each other. You have a place to belong.

# THE WELL

Are you thirsty, are you searching?
Are you longing for his mercy?

Come to the well, drink living water.
Come and be filled with the love of the Father.
Wherever you are, wherever you've been,
Come to the well, never thirst again.

Bring your worry, all your hurting,
To the place where grace is flowing.

Come to the well, drink living water.
Come and be filled with the love of the Father.
Wherever you are, wherever you've been,
Come to the well, never thirst again.

Come as you are, as you are, come.

—Michael Boggs/Jeremy Johnson

# Reflections

❧ How do the words of "The Well" connect with your life?

❧ God came to Hagar in the wilderness. How does God come to you in your wilderness?

❧ How would you answer God's question, "Where are you going? What are you doing?"

❧ Jesus spoke the truth about the life of the woman at the well. If Jesus told the truth about your life, what would he say?

❧ In what ways do you identify with the woman at the well?

❧ Describe how you believe God feels about you. Be honest.

❧ Who are the people standing by ready to accept you and support you if you would let them?

# AUTHENTICITY

We invite you to exchange the familiar for the extraordinary.
It's worth the risk.

# 6

# NOTHING CAN SEPARATE ME

*Being real means you can expect God in hard times.*

I wanted a baby again.

After our loss and my panic attacks, in my tenacious way, I climbed back to life. In addition to the family business and my work for Cliff Richard, Bob and I got involved with youth ministry at our church. I was always looking for diversions, a reason not to lose myself in the cloud constantly waiting for me.

In time, I was ready to try to have another baby, and I conceived. For the first few months, the pregnancy was typical. I loved being pregnant! Most days I couldn't hold *anything* down until early afternoon, but the hormonal upheaval of pregnancy seemed to clear my brain. Mentally I had never felt better. The baby was doing well as I moved through the stages of pregnancy.

Then one day the flutters stopped.

I went to the doctor, who did an ultrasound and assured me the baby was fine. Relieved when I started to feel the baby move again, I got ready to start Lamaze classes and prepare for delivery. I thought everything was back to normal. When I stepped on a scale at a check-up, however, I had gained ten pounds in just two weeks.

"Are you feeling itchy?" the nurse asked me.

"Yes," I answered, wondering how she would know that.

She took my blood pressure and calmly commented it was a little high, so they would need to do some more tests. A monitor assured me the baby was fine, but the doctor came in and explained that I would have to go to the hospital. My blood pressure was more than a little high; the nurse likely had been trying to keep me calm by not making a big deal of the reading, but this was the beginning of preeclampsia, sometimes referred to as toxemia, a serious condition that occurs in late pregnancy.

"What does that mean?" I wanted to know.

"If we can't get the pressure down," the doctor explained, "we'll need to induce labor or do a C-section to prevent a stroke. If you're in distress, the baby is in distress."

I listened in disbelief.

"You should probably call your husband," the doctor advised.

I did call Bob, and we went to the hospital where they gave me some medication but said that if the pressure did not come down within two hours, they would induce labor.

It came down.

But for nearly two months, I got to lie in bed at home on my left side. It was either that or stay in the hospital for all those weeks. I went every other day for stress tests to see how the baby was doing. In six weeks, I gained thirty-five pounds just lying in bed doing nothing. I suppose most of us would welcome a couple of days of lying around not doing much of anything, but almost two months of this, while worried about my baby, was a different story.

I had a lot of time to think in those weeks. If I lived, I lived. If I died, I died. That's what I thought about. And either way, it would be okay. The apostle Paul's words at the end of Romans 8 flooded my mind as I parked my soul in that passage during bed rest.

*Can anything ever separate us from Christ's love? Does it mean he no longer loves us if we have trouble or calamity, or are persecuted, or hungry, or destitute, or in danger or threatened with death? . . . No, despite all these things, overwhelming victory is ours through Christ, who loved us.*

*And I am convinced that nothing can ever separate us from God's love. Neither death nor life, neither angels nor demons, neither our fears for today nor our worries about tomorrow—not even the powers of hell can separate us from God's love. No power in the sky above or in the earth below—indeed, nothing in all creation will ever be able to separate us from the love of God that is revealed in Christ Jesus our Lord.* (Romans 8:35, 37–39)

During those long weeks, God was saying to me that it was important I understand nothing could separate me from him. *Nothing.* A difficult pregnancy—or its possible devastating outcomes—could not separate me from Christ's love. If I lived, I lived. And if I died, I died. And it would be okay.

## Receive God's gift of real people.

When all this was going on, I began to receive cards of encouragement from a man named Dan Meininger. Dan had filled in for our vacationing pastor occasionally and affirmed me one Sunday morning when I offered special music. I always enjoyed his messages, but I did not know him well, so his cards were a pleasant surprise. Dan did not know a lot about the people in our church, but God seemed to bring to his mind the names of four couples in the congregation. I did not realize at the time that meeting Dan Meininger would change my life almost as profoundly as having a baby.

Our daughter, Jillian, was born healthy, but apparently she was fed up with what she had been through. My blood pressure shot up during delivery, so it was a tense time for everyone involved. When the hospital staff put Jillian on the table to assess her APGAR scores, as they do for all newborns immediately after birth, she looked at me with an expression of disapproval I found humorously puzzling from a newborn. But she was healthy, and a few minutes later she was placed in my arms. If you were to meet Jillian, you would not be surprised at her initial reactions. She is very capable of communicating what's on her mind. She's intelligent and beautiful, with an unusual God-given confidence that was even apparent at less than an hour old.

Now it was time to adjust. The troubles certainly were not over. As sure as I was that nothing could separate me from the love of Christ, I continued in a mode of being functionally depressed. The baby did not eat well, which added stress. I still didn't want to present myself to the world, and now I had the perfect excuse, a new baby. I could stay home with my little girl, which many people expected would happen, at least for a few weeks.

Little did I know what was happening in Dan Meininger's life at the same time. Dan had a ministry of encouragement and a vibrant, intuitive prayer life. He had these faces of four couples on his mind to pray for, and he wanted to know more about the people. When he looked through a pictorial directory of our congregation, he realized that the four couples on his heart were involved in youth ministry. Dan approached our pastor about taking the four couples on an overnight retreat to encourage them and explore their ministry.

So there I was, with a newborn who was not eating, postpartum issues that aggravated my tendency toward depression, and a relative stranger who wanted my husband and me to spend a weekend with him.

As unlikely as it sounds, I went. Jillian was only a month old at the time of this retreat, but my mom was more than capable of tending to our little "splendid lady," as we called her. The retreat center was only forty-five minutes from home. Others encouraged me to take the opportunity to sleep through the night!

Meeting Dan added a dimension to my life that I had not realized was missing. Dan became a spiritual dad to me. He opened up my heart to the spiritual and emotional aspects of God's heart for me, and for other women, too. For the longest time, my spirituality was very Jesus-focused. I was comfortable with Jesus. He was the faithful suitor who didn't jerk me around. Now I began to see the fatherhood of God. In the months that followed, my understanding of God's love for me deepened. I wasn't female by accident. Being a woman was not somehow second class. God loved me and created me female for a purpose. He is *my* Father. I have a place in his family just the way I am. It doesn't matter if I don't have the same tastes or the identical politics or philosophy as everyone else in God's family. It's still a family, and I still have a place.

Your earthly father may have disappointed you and even made you leery of the word *father*. Or perhaps he was a dependable provider for your physical needs but just never connected emotionally. If something like this happened to you, it could be painful. It may be hard to see God as a good, emotionally engaged Father. Satan stole something from you, but God can give it back in abundance. Your place to belong is waiting for you.

I call God my dad now. Whether you embrace the beauty of the word or painful emotions flood your soul when you hear it, there is a perfect father. Some folks get a tad uncomfortable when I refer to God as "Dad." At times I call him "Father," a term of respect and deep awe. But he's also Dad, the one to whom I go when the world is unfair or when I have done something stupid or scraped my emotional knees. He is the one who saves every tear I've cried.

When our daughter Jillian was about three years old, Bob and I loaded up the car and decided we would visit the East Coast. As we crossed the southern border of Maine, driving along the coastline, Jillian needed to stretch her little legs. A playground overlooking a breathtaking rocky beach was the perfect spot. Below us ocean waves crashed against the rocks, and above us gulls whirled and made their signature sound. The salty sea air filled my lungs. But even more memorable than the landscape was the vision of my husband loving our little girl, her heart soaring as she enjoyed being the apple of her daddy's eye. She laughed and beamed her splendid smile while her daddy swung her back and forth on that stunning September day. When I need a visual in my mind of what a daddy is and how God feels about me, I remember that day.

God treasures me. He treasures you, too.

## Look for God in real life.

Around the time Jillian was born and I met Dan, I read a book that had been sitting around the house for weeks. My sister-in-law, Carol, gave the book to my husband as a gift, but it turned out that God meant the book for me. In addition to not eating very well, Jillian was not a great napper.

But she would relax for periods of time, and one day I picked up this book as something to read while the baby was calm and resting. After weeks of being coffee table décor, now this book opened my eyes to something I needed to see all along. Max Lucado's *The Great House of God* explores the theme of intimacy and relationship with God through the Lord's Prayer. I saw in this book how much God wants me to draw close to him—to live with him, to have a place in his house and in his family.

My life was changing all at once. Through a difficult pregnancy, I knew nothing could separate me from Christ's love. Through Dan, I gained a new picture of the fatherhood of God. And through a simple book that God placed in my home before I realized I needed it, I had a new vision of what intimacy with God could be like.

God allows you to be uniquely who you are. In fact, he *wants* you to be who you are. He created you. Your place in his family does not depend on comparing yourself to everyone else in the family. It doesn't depend on being good enough to belong. It doesn't depend on getting everything exactly right. God calls you to him and gives you a place to belong. He invites you to step inside, to be close to him, to experience his fatherly love for you. *You* can be the child on the swing basking in your Father's love.

This happens in the midst of real life. The invitation to be intimate with God does not flutter down from the sky on a calm day when nothing else seems to be happening in your life. It breaks in and through those moments when you need it most. If times are hard for you, expect God. Look for him.

> *I was convinced I just didn't belong. Connecting with women had never been easy, and I had an aversion to women's events. I struggled to relate to the people speaking. If someone appeared too "perfect," it probably wasn't true and I couldn't trust her. Yes, the core issue was trust. Can I trust you to love me as I am? In Circle of Friends, I found real women who aren't perfect but serve a God who is perfect. Their transparency is refreshing, their friendship is sincere, and they accept me as I am. Only God can be all things to me—my hope, my salvation, the love of my life, and the one who will never disappoint. But he brought these women into my life to reveal a new dimension of his love and healing to me. —Dawn*

God is not waiting around for you to be perfect before you can belong to him. He invites you to be real, and in being real—in an intimate relationship with him just as you are—you see where you belong.

# 7

# MIDNIGHT PRAYERS AND
# WATERSHED MOMENTS

*Being real means you can respond to the important moments.*

Two years after my daughter's birth, I stood in my ordinary kitchen and experienced something extraordinary. The sliding glass door streamed the sunlit blue sky onto my countertops. I stood at the sink, surrounded by light cherry stained cabinets and walls papered with tiny blue and peach flowers. The sun was so bright I felt warmth from its presence. The particles floating in the air were like God shining brightly into my kitchen as if to say, "Can you see what I have for you?"

The question was legitimate, because I struggled with that very issue.

On the one hand, my heart was in a perpetual state of expectancy. God was bringing hurting women across my path. Just looking into their faces and listening to what was in their hearts, I knew I had found my ministry calling. God wanted me to be available to encourage women and help them trust that forgiveness and deliverance were available. They had a purpose in life. God would use them. Music would be a part of my ministry to other women, and they would find their ministries as well.

On the other hand, my spirit felt condemned. While my desire to worship the Lord musically was at the forefront of my mind, I heard Satan saying, "Are you kidding me? Do you really think God is going to use you?

After what you've done? Why do you think anyone would want to hear anything you have to say? Why do you have the arrogance to think you make a difference after you have done these things? If people only knew."

Even as I stood in expectancy before God about the ministry he would unfold in my life, I was in a state of interior devastation. The enemy was doing his best to get me to run in the other direction because of the shame of what happened to me as a teenager and the mistakes I had made as a result of that experience.

The thing that made me most angry with myself was that recently I had read a book about people who made poor choices and moved through them toward healing, but for some reason I told myself, *That can't be me. It doesn't apply to me.*

Every day I opened the Word of God, and he showed me wonderful things about himself and the love and forgiveness he offered me and other women. I couldn't wait to read the next thing he was going to show me. But every day the combination of my emotional ill health with untreated depression tortured my spirit. Everything hurt. Either I was going to follow the Lord and believe what he did for the woman at the well in Samaria—and that he could do it for me and other women—or I was going to give in to the lies that invaded my heart.

## HEAR HIS VOICE TODAY.

On that vivid, streaming morning in my kitchen, the intensity of my hatred for the enemy was just as black as the sun was bright. I knew that this moment was important to me, for good or for bad. Hebrews 4:7 came to mind: "Today when you hear his voice, don't harden your hearts." If I allowed Satan to overwhelm me, I hated to think what would happen. God was speaking to me, and I wanted more than anything to listen to what he said. This moment, standing at the sink, mattered for the rest of my life.

I called Dan, my spiritual father. By now we had known each other for a couple of years. He knew my past and my mistakes. He knew what weighed me down.

"Did you read your e-mail this morning?" Dan asked on the phone.

"No," I answered.

"Go read your e-mail," he said. "The Lord woke me up last night, and I prayed for you for hours."

As I read Dan's message, the words of Psalm 25, and some commentary on what it meant, I was at a crossroads. I wanted to trust God. I prayed, *Please, God, you've told me what I believe you want me to do. You know everything I've ever done, so don't let me be disgraced by my past. Don't let the devil steal away from me what you have given.*

This was a watershed moment, a dividing point in my life and ministry. Dan loved me enough to pray through the night and send me a word of encouragement that gave me hope. His message moved me from sitting in the pit of condemnation to a vision of dwelling in the secret place of the Most High God. Psalm 25 planted principles in my heart that have sustained me through the years and set the direction for my ministry with other women.

## WHEN THE MOMENT COMES, BE REAL.

We all have those watershed moments. How we respond to them can change the stories of our lives, for better or for worse, and the stories of the lives of the people we meet and interact with. Perhaps even as you read about my watershed moment, you thought of one of your own.

One temptation is to give in to the lies of the enemy and believe that mistakes in your past will determine your future. Shame can be overwhelming, a black cloud that you cannot see your way through. It slaps you in the face every time you lift your gaze. You may feel in your gut that you already ruined your life—or that someone else ruined it for you—and that's the end of the story. What's done is done, and you can't undo it. This is going to be "normal" for you from now on.

And then you think that if you don't talk about it, perhaps it won't matter so much. You can't change what happened, but the world doesn't have to know all about it. Perhaps you've learned to go to church and smile and quote the Bible verses. You may even be part of a Bible study group or ministry team, but no one knows your deepest feelings. No one knows the lies Satan whispers in your ears between your prayers. You've learned that digging deep causes pain, so it's easier to live on the surface.

Some choices do have natural consequences that we cannot escape. Perpetual shame is not one of them. You do not have to live your life with two faces—the one other people see and the one you look at in the mirror. By God's grace, you have another option. Be real. Be genuine. Be authentic.

As unhealthy as the patterns of our lives may be, they become familiar. At least we have some idea how to function within those boun-daries. Authenticity is a risk. We have to trade the familiar for the unfamiliar with the hope that what lies ahead is extraordinary.

What is your watershed moment? Perhaps you are standing in that moment even right now, the moment where you will *shush* the enemy and turn toward the voice of God—today. Today you will listen to his voice.

Be real with God. Start there. Then be real with one other person in your life. Recognize the important moments of your life and hear God's voice calling you in the midst of them.

> *I think it is essential and almost humorous to explain just how different each member of our circle truly is. We have four distinct personalities that bring interest and diversity to our group. Maybe that is why we never get tired of getting together. The thinker in our group challenges us to look deeper into the meaning of situations and God's Word. The compassionate one keeps us in check as to how our words and actions affect others. The lighthearted one keeps us laughing and makes sure we gather even when it would be easier for everyone to go on with her busy schedule. And the last member would be me, who finds it hard to beat around the bush. For better or worse, we are who we are.*
> *—Joyce*

# 8

# On the Mountain

*Being real means you stand on a sure foundation.*

When I got off the phone with Dan on that shimmering June day, I immersed myself in Psalm 25. The faith of David the psalmist challenged mine. If I act as if everything has always been perfect in a flowery, synthetic way, I'm fooling myself. For God to use me, I had to lay down my pride and be transparent. It was time to stop trying to deceive people into thinking I was something I was not. All these years later, Psalm 25 is still a powerful passage in my relationship with the Lord. It cries out with the words of my own heart, and at the same time echoes the words of God for me.

Embracing Psalm 25 as my own was the beginning of reaching out to other women to encourage real relationship with God and each other. Walk with me through this psalm and discover the riches it holds for you.

## Give God your shame.

*O LORD, I give my life to you. I trust in you, my God! Do not let me be disgraced, or let my enemies rejoice in my defeat. No one who trusts in you will ever be disgraced, but disgrace comes to those who try to deceive others.* (Psalm 25:1–3)

David is well aware that his enemies will jump on his weaknesses. He knows people are waiting to laugh at him, to celebrate when he fails. Even with all that going on, his starting point is trust in God.

As I read these opening verses, my heart ached with their truth for me. I wanted to trust God. I wanted to give my life to him. I believed he had told me I would have a ministry encouraging women, but I prayed along with David, *Don't let the devil steal away from me what you gave. Don't let me be disgraced by my past.*

Where is your starting point going into your troubles? Do you hear God speaking to you or the enemy whispering in your ear?

## GOD SHOWS THE WAY.

*Show me the right path, O LORD; point out the road for me to follow. Lead me by your truth and teach me, for you are the God who saves me. All day long I put my hope in you. Remember, O LORD, your compassion and unfailing love, which you have shown from long ages past. Do not remember the rebellious sins of my youth. Remember me in the light of your unfailing love, for you are merciful, O LORD.* (Psalm 25:4–7)

David knows he is not journeying alone. God is on the journey with him and ready to point the way when David feels lost. God's love lights the way. What a comfort to know you are not walking the path blindly! God is there to show the right way, point out the road, lead in truth, teach, and save. God's *unfailing* love provides the light you need to see where you are going. I see in these verses the importance of knowing what the Word of God says. Imperfect people show up all over the Bible, warts and all, but God's grace abounds in their imperfections. That means his grace can abound in my imperfections as well, and yours. You might mess things up, but you can count on God to be in the middle of straightening them out again. When you lose hope in yourself, you still have hope in God. He'll dust you off and stand you on your feet, point, and say, "That's the way to go. Stay on the path."

## Learn from God's faithfulness.

*The LORD is good and does what is right; he shows the proper path to those who go astray. He leads the humble in doing right, teaching them his way. The LORD leads with unfailing love and faithfulness all who keep his covenant and obey his demands. For the honor of your name, O LORD, forgive my many, many sins. Who are those who fear the LORD? He will show them the path they should choose. They will live in prosperity, and their children will inherit the land. The LORD is a friend to those who fear him. He teaches them his covenant. My eyes are always on the LORD, for he rescues me from the traps of my enemies.* (Psalm 25:8–15)

All this talk about the proper path and being humble and keeping a covenant obeying God's demands might sound legalistic. It's not! It's the heart of love and protection. David understands that. He is part of the people of Israel, with whom God made a covenant of love long before David was on the scene. It goes back to the days of the promise that Abraham would have a son. Generations later, David sees the power of covenant.

When I look at my wedding band, I don't see a reminder of legalism or bondage. I see a reminder of a covenant I made with my husband, a covenant I fully want to keep. For whatever reason in the grace and mercy of God—not because I deserve it more than other women—God gave me a husband who taught me the love of Christ. Bob could have deserted me when times got hard, but he didn't. Some people thought I had already gone off the deep end at my wedding because I chose to say "love, honor, and *obey*." But I knew I needed to say that last word. If I didn't trust Bob enough to obey him, why was I even marrying him in the first place? I knew our covenant together would be a place of love and protection.

If you live in a neighborhood with a homeowners association, you know the rules about fences and antennas and clotheslines that break the neighborhood covenant. Actually, a covenant is not so much about what you are *not* allowed to do as it is about the promises of what you *will* do. A covenant is not about rules, but about promises. And God keeps his promises. I know that even something as simple as looking at a wedding band can be difficult for women who don't feel comfort at the sight. Instead of love and protection, they may see disappointment and betrayal. Even if you do not have the kind of husband I have, you have God. He leads you with unfailing love and faithfulness. God is not faithful to me and at the same time unfaithful to you. What kind of faithfulness would that be?

You've heard enough of my story to know I don't live in la-la land. I'm well aware of the sharp edges that rip up the fabric of our lives. I know that faith in God does not put some sort of protective dome around me so that bad stuff never happens. There are things in this life we will never be able to explain because our knowledge is finite. But along with David the psalmist, I know that God is there with me, whatever happens. God gives us the faith to trust him even in things we don't understand.

Can you put yourself in God's hands and believe he will keep his promise of *unfailing* love?

I love the sense of promise in verse 13: "They will live in prosperity, and their children will inherit the land." I see God's hand at work in my family's history and know that the past touches the future. Both my parents and my grandparents came to faith well into their adult years. My parents were in their thirties, and my grandparents even a generation older. My maternal grandfather was eighty years old when a local pastor reached out to him. I was about eight when he was baptized. I can still see him in his white robe.

> *Circle of Friends has blessed my life in so many ways. I have fun friends who encourage me and help me through the obstacles of life. What a gift! I learn so much from these special ladies. Now I want to go out and help others too. —JoEllen*

God's chronology might not be as straightforward as ours. If you look at the facts and dates of my family's history, you might not think I had a Christian heritage. But God used a local church and a pastor to give me a retroactive Christian heritage. Bob's side of the family has a long history of Christian faith, but my children have a Christian heritage on my side as well, because in God's timing, he brought my grandparents to Himself during their final seasons of life. My children are receiving the grace that God brought to my family in his own time. He is in control even when we don't realize it.

I want to be God's friend. And I want God to be my friend (verse 14). I want to take God into my confidence and pour out my heart to him and hear what he has to say to me. On Facebook you can "friend" somebody with a click. Now the person can read whatever you choose to reveal about yourself in an electronically public place—your Facebook "wall"—and tease you or congratulate you or make funky comments. But we all know that is not the stuff of true friendship. In this psalm, David reminds us to be the kind of person who is godly, the kind of person others can tell their secrets to and know that you will be as careful with the information as if you were holding precious stones. This kind of authentic relationship with other people begins in our experience with God.

What kind of speaking terms are you on with God? Do you post a comment every now and then, or do you trust him with your secrets?

## LOOK TO GOD FOR HOPE.

*Turn to me and have mercy, for I am alone and in deep distress. My problems go from bad to worse. Oh, save me from them all! Feel my pain and see my trouble. Forgive all my sins. See how many enemies I have and how viciously they hate me! Protect me! Rescue my life from them! Do not let me be disgraced, for in you I take refuge. May integrity and honesty protect me, for I put my hope in you.* (Psalm 25:16–21)

David is known and loved by many, but he has enemies as well. David makes mistakes. Sometimes he goes on a bit of a power trip. He is the person God chose to be the next king of Israel, but he waits many years to get the job. During those years, plenty of people try to make sure it will never happen—including Saul, the reigning king. David does some stupid things and he admits it. But he also suffers unfairly at the hands of others. We see in this psalm David's sense of his problems going from bad to worse, and he appeals to God for help. "Feel my pain and see my trouble!"

Most of us don't have to go far outside our own environments to find someone who doesn't like us. It may even be that the people we spend most of our time with don't like us all that well, such as in the workplace. The same was true for David. His very real physical enemies—the soldiers of the current king, Saul—were always in the next cave or wrapped in the next shadow. Satan taunts us with these realities in the hope that we'll just give up. David knows what it is like to live at this edge. He does not believe he can simply protect himself. He can't just keep hanging on in his own strength. He knows he needs God. That is the bottom line. David asks God to wrap him in a cloak of integrity as he faces his problems.

We have the same opportunity to walk in obedience. I think about my life before I was intentional about reading God's love letters to me and the rest of his family, and I honestly wonder how I could be satisfied with the life I was living. I wasn't! But neither was I diligently seeking out God's plan. Now it's a whole different story.

If you do your part and seek after God, he will reward you with the information and revelation you need to walk in your calling. Don't let the enemy distract you or discourage you with problems piling on problems. Follow David's example and keep your hope steadfast in God.

## GOD CARES FOR ALL HIS PEOPLE.

*O God, ransom Israel from all its troubles.* (Psalm 25:22)

David finishes his psalm by thinking about other people. He pleads for God to save not just him from whatever his trouble is at the time, but to save all God's people from all their troubles. That's a bold prayer!

This is the big picture. David is dealing with his own sin and struggles in his own relationship with God. But the story comes back to the big picture—"God, help your people!" Even as we work on our own individual issues, the body of Christ must be concerned about the health of the whole, not just the health of one cell. As we pray for our own health—physically, spiritually, emotionally—we must pray for the health of everyone around us.

I have a calling—and so do you. What we do is not just for ourselves, but for the glory of God and for all the people our lives touch every day. I think of my daughter, who is a teenager now. In thirty years, when she is the age I am now, what kind of world will she be living in? Will her community have a woman in it with a desire to make a difference in the lives of women in that community? Will there be someone who wants to make a place for Jillian to belong? And will Jillian be the kind of woman who makes a place for someone else to belong? Will she be a godly friend because she is God's friend? I am laying the groundwork for the world my children will live in. My mother-in-law invested in her community, and my mother invested in employees with sick children. Those choices affected me, and I want God's impact on my life to affect the women who will be my daughter's friends in the decades to come.

Your life touches so many other lives, whether you realize it or not. You can be Facebook friends and just sort of keep tabs on the outer workings of the lives of people you know, or you can choose to dig deep and get real. David got real with God because he knew God was not going to change.

Love.

Mercy.

Forgiveness.

Truth.

Covenant.

Hope.

Deliverance.

These things are not going anywhere, because they are rooted in the character of God. If that's not a foundation for real living, I don't know what is. Put yourself in the middle of Psalm 25 alongside David. Look out from the grid of your own troubles, the daily pressures, the disappointments, or persisting pain, and see that God wants to deliver you from them. If you're standing on a mountaintop at the moment and things are looking good, you can be sure a valley is in your future. Are you ready for it? If you're trapped in a valley and can't find your way out, lift your eyes to the mountain. There's the way out—the mountain that does not shift, the mountain that is God.

# 9

# RISKING REAL

*Being real means you can invite others to complete your circle.*

Throw a stone in a lake and it makes ripples. The same is true for our lives. Each one of us is a pebble of influence, stirring up circles when we throw ourselves into authentic living and ministry. But if we want the circle to be complete and strong, we have to risk being real.

Very soon after the June morning in my kitchen, I lived through an illustration of this truth. An old friend and I planned to go to a women's conference where my friend Lisa Harper was speaking. At that time, Lisa was the director of women's outreach at Focus on the Family. I'd known the woman I was going to the conference with since I was a teenager. She was a badly needed positive influence in my life in those days. Later, when I was on bed rest while pregnant with my daughter, my friend visited and brought food and cared for me. More recently, though, we had drifted apart. She showed an attitude that I perceived as condescending toward me, as if I were a little sister who didn't know what she knew, and I struggled against anger and frustration. Now we were going to spend hours together in the car driving to this conference, and I wasn't sure what to expect.

Before our trip, I dreamed about my friend. We were eating a meal in a restaurant near where we lived, but outside the streets were like Manhattan—busy, noisy, and overwhelming. In the dream, my friend was pregnant and she suddenly started to swell up.

"You have toxemia," I said.

"I think I'm dying," she responded.

In the dream, she couldn't walk, so I carried her up the hill to a hospital and walked down the corridor. She didn't seem to weigh anything. At the end of the hall was her husband, dressed in scrubs.

God seemed to say to me, "You brought her here, and now she needs to deal with this with him."

My simmering irritation cooled, and I was burdened to pray for my friend instead. I pondered Romans 12:9. I like *The Message* translation of this verse: "Love from the center of who you are; don't fake it. Run for dear life from evil; hold on for dear life to good. Be good friends who love deeply; practice playing second fiddle." I had taken a turn toward risking authenticity in my life, despite the events of the past. But I had a feeling my friend was not in the same place. The dream suggested I could have a part in helping her move to a new level in her relationship with God, but I had no idea what it might look like. I just knew we were going to be alone in the car together for a long time.

On the morning of our drive, my friend was cheerful. "This is going to be so much fun!" I wasn't quite as sure "fun" was the word to describe it, but I was grateful that I felt peace from the Lord about the weekend ahead.

## IT'S YOUR CHOICE.

When Bunny Wilson, a well-known speaker at women's conferences, presented, she spoke about hiding hard things that have happened in our lives. I could sense Bunny's talk was working on my friend.

A pretty Latina woman sat near us during the event. We had never met before, and I don't know her name or where she is from. At one point she left the seating area of the arena but soon came back up and spoke to me.

"The Lord told me to tell you that your friend will tell you tonight what is going on."

I was dumbfounded but thankful for the encouragement. We never said more than, "Hello," but the Lord graciously spoke through her.

When the evening was over, my friend and I sat for a full forty-five minutes after everyone else had left the arena. I suppose I was waiting for some big revelation, but I did not know how it would come. We spent these moments in a "holy ground" silence, as if the Lord has placed a cover over both our mouths. I focused on loving from the center and reminding myself that I was not going to be fake with this friend.

Finally, she said, "Do you want to get something to eat?"

"Sure," I answered. Perhaps she would tell me at the restaurant.

Nope. We ate, went back to our room, talked to our husbands on the phone, and caught up on what was going on with our children. It got later and later. We talked like we always talked, but no great revelation came. Finally it was almost two in the morning, and I thought perhaps she would tell me what was going on during our ride home the next day.

Suddenly my friend began to weep, a deep, painful crying, and I felt as if I was just supposed to be there with her.

After a while, she said, "You know something, don't you?"

"I've been praying for you," I said softly.

My friend, whom I had known for well over a decade, opened up and told me the story of a very difficult childhood, one I never would have imagined. I had never heard this before. So many things I wondered about over the years made sense now. I found myself randomly crying for her at moments, but I felt peace in my efforts to be available for her.

"I want to deal with this," she said, "and you have to keep me accountable."

I nodded. I knew. If she was going to risk being real, she needed someone to remind her to keep moving forward.

"How did you know?" she asked. "What did that lady say to you when she came back?"

"She said you would share something with me tonight. See how much the Lord loved you so my heart would be ready?"

The next morning, my friend was different. Our relationship seemed to change. The shadow of condescension I'd been feeling in recent months was gone. My friend wanted to talk to a pastoral counselor.

After a few days passed, I called her and asked, "Did you call the counselor?" I was keeping her accountable, just as she asked me to do.

"I talked to my husband, and we decided it wouldn't be necessary," she answered.

Her mind was made up. The window had closed. We never spoke of it again. When we saw each other in a social setting soon after that pivotal moment of opportunity, she wouldn't even let me catch her eye. After a profound moment of truth together, our relationship reverted to a social and surface level. After a while, my friend and her husband withdrew from our common social circles, seeming to isolate themselves further.

She had her moment, and she couldn't do it. My heart ached for her. As far as I know, she never dealt with the pain of her past and the imprint it left on her life. Despite what she said to me in the middle of the night in a valley of tears, she did not want me to keep her accountable, not really.

Perhaps you know her fear. It's a risky thing to disturb the status quo of your life. You may have worked for years to get everything into a manageable balance, and if you touch one piece, everything else will rattle and move as well. It might all collapse, and what will you be left with?

It's a risk.

We can't have a well-rounded life without real relationships—including accountability. We need people who encourage us to take the risks. We need to be people who encourage others to risk authenticity.

When a stone drops into a lake, it first makes a small circle, then larger and larger circles. Your smallest circle of friends are the people closest to you and with whom you experience deep intimacy. Then circles open up and bring in more people, making room for others to belong.

I talk to a lot of people on the radio, but I still want to be talking to one person. We all want to feel like somebody has time for us. As people risk being real and move to stronger levels of health within themselves, they have healthy relationships that reproduce in the lives of other people. How can I expect someone to want to be honest with me unless I'm willing to do it? I'm not suggesting that you expose personal situations for the sake of shaming anybody or to make people feel sorry for you. But if you are going to grow through the experiences of your life with the certainty that God will not abandon you, other people can help. God never meant for you to be alone.

Trust is a huge thing. Not everybody deserves your trust, but someone does. God certainly does. Life gets better the more open you are. All that energy you devote to protecting yourself or hiding the truth from others can go into chasing after joy in your life.

## WE ARE ALL THE SAME.

About ten years after the Focus on the Family conference, when Circle of Friends Ministries was up and running, we were having our own annual conferences. One year our keynote speaker was Carol Kent, who tells her gripping story in her books *When I Lay My Isaac Down* and *A New Kind of Normal*. Her son killed his wife's former husband because he thought the man was a threat to their young daughters. He is serving a life sentence in prison. This is not something their family ever would have predicted, but they are walking every day by faith. Before her son's arrest, Carol says, if she heard a story of tragedy, she felt compassion but was likely to spout a Bible verse. She did not truly try to get into the person's world. The grief was something that happened outside of her.

Now she knows.

Carol and her husband spend their Sunday afternoons waiting in line for two hours for a few minutes of visiting with their son. She meets so many people of diverse backgrounds in the waiting line. Most of them never expected to be there. The experience of having a loved one in prison is a leveling experience. Whatever the particular circumstances, everybody in the line shares a common grief, a common jolt to their lives. They're all there for the same reason.

Carol Kent is an educated, sophisticated woman who never thought she would spend her Sunday afternoons at a correctional institution visiting her son. She was in the restroom one week when she heard a devastated woman sob, "I hate this place! I hate this place!" Carol knew exactly how she felt. They stood in that bathroom weeping and embracing.

As Carol spoke at our conference, she acknowledged that each person has a unique story. "What have you had to let go of?" she asked. "What have you had to embrace?" She invited women to come forward to the altar for prayer as they wrestled with the answers to these questions and face the reality of their own new kind of normal.

As part of our conference planning, we had women standing at the altar ready to receive those who came forward. We intentionally selected women we knew had a heart to intercede or offer comfort. One of the women appointed to pray has an Alpha and Omega tattoo on her forearm. As I was leading the worship music during this invitation time, I saw an Amish woman come forward. She would not have heard about our conference through her usual Amish circles. Instead, she heard about it by listening to my program on Moody Radio while working as a caregiver to her elderly employer. When this conservative Amish woman came forward for prayer, the woman waiting to embrace her was the one with the tattoo.

This is what Circle of Friends is all about. Whether you drive a horse and buggy or have a tattoo, in Christ we are all the same. We're sisters. Jesus is the center. No denominational labels divide us at that point. We comfort each other with the comfort God has given us.

We welcome you into our ministry via the radio, a website, conferences, and music. But I also challenge you to ask yourself two questions about a circle of friends right where you live.

How will you respond when someone comes to you, ready to risk being real?

Who in your life can you risk being real with?

# 10

# Jesus the Defender

*Being real means you let Jesus see you.*

Being real is a little like being naked. Okay, maybe more than a little. Clothing hides our imperfections and the most private parts of our bodies. We try on clothes before we buy them, not just to see if they fit but also to assess how they make us look. Too fat? Too short? Too pale? Too exposed? Without clothing—naked—it all hangs out for everyone to see, and for most of us that is not a comfortable feeling.

When it comes to relationships, we protect ourselves in similar ways. We keep our secrets covered. We arrange our lives so our private struggles are not exposed. We keep people at a distance so we have to face neither the judgment we fear they will throw at us nor the truth they might challenge us with. And we convince ourselves it's better that way.

It's not.

## Jesus is not the accuser.

John, the writer of the fourth gospel in the New Testament, tells us about a woman who felt exposed. Jesus was teaching one day when the Jewish religious leaders manhandled a woman to the front of the crowd and interrupted Jesus.

"Teacher," they said to Jesus, "this woman was caught in the act of adultery. The law of Moses says to stone her. What do you say?" (John 8:4–5).

Not only had the woman's sin been exposed to the religious leaders—who seemed to protect the man involved—but now they humiliated her by parading her in front of a crowd. Everybody knew! They humiliated her even further by using her as bait to trap Jesus. She was not a person to them. She was a convenient tool to use for their own purpose, which was to get Jesus to say something that could get him in trouble. She stood exposed before the crowd with fingers of accusation pointing directly at her. How could anyone be more shamed than this woman was at that moment?

If Jesus said, "Don't stone her," he would go against God's law given through Moses.

If Jesus said, "Stone her," he would defy the Romans, who ruled the region and did not allow the Jews to use their own death sentence.

But Jesus was onto their schemes, and he was not about to let this vulnerable woman pay the price for the Pharisees' manipulative games.

"Stone her," he said, "but let those who have never sinned throw the first stones."

The accusers had no choice but to walk away. One by one they slipped off until Jesus was alone with the woman in the middle of the watching crowd.

"Did even one of them accuse you?" he asked her.

"No, Lord."

"Neither do I. Go and sin no more" (John 8:11).

Even at our most vulnerable moments, Jesus is our defender. He is not the accuser. He is the vindicator. When those who are evil are out to accuse us and use us for their own agendas, Jesus is not accusing. Even if we're caught in a mistake, Jesus is not the accuser. In kindness he allows us to change. Forgiveness is just a moment away. Jesus is not there to set us up, to hurt us. He's there to help, to set free.

Even when we are at our worst, Jesus is always at his best. We're all naked in front of him. He sees everything. Let's not deceive ourselves into thinking we can hide anything from him. When we are fully exposed, his kindness and mercy overwhelm.

When I wrote the song "Beautiful," this was the situation in my mind.

One of the lines is, "You wrap my shame up in Your love for me." In that moment of forgiveness, of being set free, the woman can see she is beautiful in the eyes of Jesus, no matter what her past.

That's the opportunity each of us has, whether anyone else knows about our sin or not. Our mistakes may be publicly exposed or privately held, but Jesus knows them and doesn't accuse.

## LIVE IN SHAME NO MORE.

Several years after I became involved in women's ministry, I was working through eating disorder issues that stemmed from having been bulimic as a teenager—when I held my secret close. I felt temptation to engage in bulimic behaviors but was facing the problem square on and refusing to let it run my life. One Sunday morning I sang in church. Afterward a woman approached me and asked if we could talk.

"Would you like to come to my house?" she asked.

"Where do you live?"

She told me.

"I'll be out that way on Tuesday," I said. "I'm going to see my counselor about my eating disorder."

"What?"

"Isn't it obvious?" I asked, gesturing to my not-svelte form.

"You're actually telling me this?" She laughed nervously. "Come after your appointment."

When I met with her in her home, she explained to me that she had lost considerable weight herself. This woman was stunning in physical appearance and had the home to match.

"I'm not happy," she confided, showing me her liquor bottles. "I drink one of these a day. I don't eat now. I just drink."

"Why do you drink?" I probed.

"I have three children," she answered softly.

I was confused. "I know your son and your daughter."

"I have three children," she said again. "I had an abortion when I was seventeen. I can't enjoy the children I have now because of what I did."

I felt at a complete loss as to what to say. I tried to maintain a relationship with her after that, but she pulled back into her shell and I didn't know how to help. She told me her secret, but the shame overwhelmed her. Because of her alcoholism, fueled by her secret shame, she lost her husband and children. Eventually, I'm glad to say, she made her peace with God, remarried, and restored her relationship with her children. But it was a hard road, because for so long she felt the enemy's accusations.

I realized how ill-equipped I was to help someone who was post-abortive. Perhaps if I had been better prepared, I would have had something to offer her at the time. Perhaps she and her family would have been spared the power of shame and instead known the open arms of Jesus much sooner. I know I should not speculate whether I could have had more impact on her, but the bottom line is that I felt unqualified to offer anything other than, "I'm sorry."

Because of this woman, I sought information and training on how to minister to post-abortive women. When I had the opportunity to travel to Detroit for a meeting with UK singer Cliff Richard and PBS television, I also took advantage of a one-day training program offered by Sydna Masse nearby. Sydna, who experienced the pain of abortion herself, now leads Ramah International, a ministry that brings God's healing touch to other women, as well as men, who suffer the pain, loss, and guilt that so often manifests after a child is aborted.

I went through the training she offered on a Saturday. The following Monday I was taping my radio programs for the entire week. The training was still fresh, and I continued to process what it meant for me and how I should use it. Did I want to talk about it on the air or not? I taped Monday's program and said nothing about abortion. I taped Tuesday's program and said nothing. When it was time to tape Wednesday's program, I felt convicted that I was supposed to talk about dealing with the guilt and shame of being post-abortive. I wanted to be sympathetic to those who had been through this experience, whatever the reasons. Many women feel they have no other option. The enemy has deceived them into believing that. They are convinced that their children are better off never being born because of the circumstances of the pregnancy.

I talked about these things on the Wednesday program and said, "Maybe somebody who is listening tonight knows what I'm talking about."

Then I began to read Psalm 51, David's psalm of confession, forgiveness, and restoration after his affair with Bathsheba and the death of the child born out of his choices. Surely David felt responsible for that child's death. But he also knew God's forgiveness.

"If you made that choice," I said into the station's microphone, "you can be forgiven."

I felt that I could not talk about something so gut-wrenching and just leave listeners hanging, so I did something I had never done before. I gave out a cell phone number over the radio waves. I carried this secondary number specifically for the ministry of Circle of Friends.

"If you need to talk about the guilt and shame of having an abortion, or if you need information, call me."

I taped that program on Monday, and it aired Wednesday night. When I was coming out of church on Wednesday night, I felt the phone vibrate. I didn't get to it fast enough. The number showed "unavailable," so I couldn't return the call, but the caller left a voice message.

> To listen to the Circle of Friends radio program daily is to get a dose of sincerity and devotion to our Lord and Savior Jesus Christ. I listen faithfully, and they always speak truth. They are sold out to God and allow Jesus to pour his love down over each one of us daily.
> —Roberta

"I heard what you said, and I know you were talking to me," she said. "I'm not sure God can forgive me, but I'm going to ask him."

*Okay, Lord, whoever that was, please be with her.*

A few days later, the phone went off again. The number again showed "unavailable," but this time I answered in time.

"I called you last week," the voice said. "I just need to talk."

She didn't even give her name. In her early thirties, she was divorced with an eight-year-old son. She got involved with a man and became pregnant.

He didn't want the baby.

"I didn't see any other way," she said. "It was the biggest mistake I ever made in my life."

The abortion had been a few weeks earlier. On Monday—the day I was taping my programs and wondering what to say—this woman was trying to stave off a nervous breakdown over what she had done. By Wednesday she was distracting herself with some painting work in her son's bedroom and turned on the radio for company.

"You were talking to me," she said. "I wept! I called you."

"Yes, I've been praying for you. What can I do to help?"

We talked for a few minutes, and then I said, "I'd like you to talk to someone more experienced than I am. Let me give you information. But stay in touch and let me know how you're doing. God does forgive you."

The woman, whose named turned out to be Jo, contacted Sydna Masse's organization. She called me again about a month later.

"I read some of the books," she said, "but I'm still having a hard time forgiving myself. I'm so depressed."

"But that's not unusual in your grief," I responded. "You're still grieving the loss of a child, even if it was because of a choice."

Jo got plugged into a support group for post-abortive women, and we stayed in touch.

About six months later I was scheduled to go to Chattanooga, Tennessee. Women's ministry speaker Lisa Harper invited several of us from Circle of Friends to a new conference format she was debuting for the ministry season. As the date approached, I told Jo about the conference.

Chattanooga hosts a National Memorial to the Unborn. People who suffer the pain of losing a child through abortion can honor the child with a plaque on the Wall of Names. When I mentioned the conference to Jo, she told me she felt the Lord had been telling her to memorialize her unborn child and she had scheduled her trip for the same time I would be going to Chattanooga. Since the timing was perfect, I invited Jo to attend the conference as well. The theme was "Every Woman's Hope." No matter where you've been or what you've done, your hope for healing and restoration is through Christ.

The trip to Chattanooga gave Jo some long-awaited closure. Yes, she made a mistake, and she regretted it deeply. But she found mercy and forgiveness at the foot of the cross. Her child is safely protected in the arms of Jesus, and Jo looks forward to an eternity-long relationship with her child because of Christ.

Abortion.

Eating disorders.

Alcoholism.

Affairs.

Abuse.

Crimes.

The list of mistakes that feed our shame is endless. But shame does not have to be endless. Whatever your situation, remember the woman in John 8. Jesus is not the accuser. Jesus is the defender. Jesus offers forgiveness. Jesus offers hope for a future wrapped in love, not shame. Jesus is the first safe person for you to stand naked in front of and name your shame aloud. Jesus is the first place where you can be real.

## 11

# PRETENDING NO MORE

*Being real means you can't pretend anymore.*

I was three years old and my sister was chasing me. I fell and ended up with a lifetime scar near one eye. Could it be removed? Probably? A plastic surgeon likely would offer several options. But I don't want it removed. It's part of who I am. There's something to be said about a scar. It's evidence of a wound that healed. Sometimes you have to clean out scar tissue, and it's painful, but the process promotes healing. And once the scar is there, you can't ever pretend the event never happened.

In contrast, Botox has wormed its way into our culture and what we think we have to look like. Just a few injections here and there can take care of the signs of normal aging or features that you've never been quite happy with.

It's fake, of course. Nothing stops the clock. We're all older than we were last week. And all the Botox or plastic surgery in the world won't erase the things that make you unique. You still have a history—and may need to deal with some of it straight on. You still have a future where you can choose to go after what brings joy to your life, rather than live in shame.

I find myself asking, what about spiritual Botox? It looks good at first, but when you get close, there's that pretending business again. Sometimes I pretend that I'm not really hurt when people accuse me of not caring, just because I see things from a different perspective. I know I'm not right all the time. Sometimes I fire before the "Ready, aim," which isn't smart. My sister LeeAnne reminds me about an episode in the now-retro television show *Happy Days*. The Fonz couldn't get himself to utter the words "I was wrong." LeeAnne often will say, "Are you doing a *Fonz*?"

Plenty of people have trouble admitting when they're wrong. They also have trouble admitting when something in their life is not what everyone thinks it is. When we put on the Botox smile and head into another day without telling ourselves or anyone else the truth, that's pretending.

If I'm singing karaoke, I might pretend to be Cher—without the wardrobe, thank you. Pretending in the sense of imagining can be fun for a moment, but then it's back to reality. Reality might or might not be fun. It might or might not be exciting. It might or might not impress other people.

But it's the truth.

I don't know about you, but I don't like pretending. Jesus said he is the truth, and the truth sets us free. Jesus invited me into his reality, where he bled, suffered, and died so that my sin and shame do not have to separate me from God.

My sister left an abusive marriage. That was a reality where pretending didn't help anything.

Pretending didn't make my friend's childhood issues go away.

Pretending didn't make Jo's pain after her abortion go away.

Pretending not to be an alcoholic doesn't remove the reason someone reaches for the bottle.

Pretending a marriage is rich and fulfilling doesn't erase the heartache that may be at its core.

Pretending you had a great year and sending out a cheery Christmas letter doesn't change reality if serious illness is screaming questions about faith at you.

So why do we keep on pretending? Why do we keep zipping our lips instead of telling ourselves the truth—or daring to tell someone else? Why do we avoid the process of seeking emotional health when we would treat a physical illness in a heartbeat, even if the treatment were painful? People with cancer undergo surgery, chemotherapy, and radiation that makes them feel pretty awful because their sights are set on healing.

Why do we keep pretending?

## Step out of the comfort zone.

When my son was six weeks old, a frightening reality confronted me abruptly. After giving Christian a bath, I took him into the bedroom to dress him. Usually I used the changing table, but that day I had laid my son down on the middle of the bed instead. Moments later, in a paralyzing panic attack, I fell to my knees, unable to move, unable to do whatever needed doing next.

What if he had been on the table and not strapped in? He was too young to crawl from the center of the bed, so he was safe there, thank the Lord. I watched him from my impaired position, grateful that he was protected from falling.

What if I had a panic attack while I was driving with both my kids in the car? The thought was sobering.

As scared as I was, I knew I had to tell my husband. I admit I had a moment's temptation to remain silent, to hide my fear and shame. But I knew I couldn't deceive him by withholding the incident. Bob said, "Are you calling Dr. Canfield, or am I?" I trusted Bob, and I trusted Dr. Canfield. Teresa Canfield is a very special woman, with a deep devotion to the health of the moms she cares for through pregnancy, delivery, and post-partum. I'm so thankful that God appointed her to be my doctor at that crucial time in my life. My usual depression was always there just below the surface. In those post-partum weeks, I could no longer mask it. The days of pretending were over. Dr. Canfield thoroughly evaluated my situation and immediately

> In the Circle of Friends, I get to be me! No masks, no pretense. It's a safe place, a place I can let down the walls guarding my heart. I found a group of ladies who love God and his Word and follow hard after him. They are running the faith race with me and helping me along the way. They've loved me by recognizing God's gifts in me and allowing me to use them, and they provide a community to encourage other women to do the same. —Missy

started me on an antidepressant medication.

I was in my comfort zone of just coping with my years of depression. The possible danger I could put my children in woke me up to reality—to the truth that I needed help. It wasn't working for me to just manage on my own.

You do have an alternative to spinning your wheels wherever you are. You can stop whatever you're doing that's getting you nowhere. How long do we drive a car with a flat tire and expect it to be a useful vehicle? If the same thing keeps happening, it's time to get out of your comfort zone.

We live in a shallow world. Shallow is comfortable. Shallow doesn't ask you to take risks. You can wade around in a pool of relationships without ever having to find out if you can swim in the deep end.

Here's what I want you to hear: Don't be afraid of the friend you could become.

Do you know the relationships you're missing in your life? Can you really find where you belong if you don't leave where you are?

The pace of modern life makes it easy to stay in the shallow end of the pool. It's a big pool. You can wade around for years and never get past your knees in the water. But if you're tired of pretending, and if you're tired of splashing around in the shallow end, let me suggest that you begin by making time for face-to-face contact with real people. Even with people we care about, we too easily justify saying e-mail is sufficient. After all, everyone is busy. Trying to match schedules and find that mutually open hour between carpools and work schedules and doctors' appointments is a daunting task. But I wonder if we teach ourselves to be emotionally void with e-mail and social media.

We miss hearing the tone in someone's voice that might alert us to something wrong.

We miss the opportunity to put a hand on someone's arm and speak a word of encouragement.

We miss the chance to meet someone's eyes and discern what might be there.

We miss the lull in conversation that might be the edge of a life-changing moment.

I have a cell phone. I send text messages. I'm on Facebook. I read e-mail. I'm not suggesting technology is inherently evil or has no place in our lives. But I am saying it's not sufficient. The loose, abbreviated style of most electronic communication is not the heart of an authentic relationship. It doesn't replace face time.

Whenever anyone makes the effort to engage me, I need to give the person my attention. Time is the most precious gift we have to give. Most people are not looking for me to have all the answers or to monopolize all my time. They just want to know that someone cares.

In a performance-driven world, we want God to be like Google— fast and full of answers. He wants us to spend time. The answers are not instantaneous. They come from spending time with God, and we share them with each other by spending time together. In the Resources section of this book, you'll find a daily reading schedule that will help you read through the entire Bible in one year. This is a structured way to develop a healthy spiritual core based on reading God's Word and knowing what it says. If you've never done that before, try it!

The experience of God's Word not only helps you find answers for your own life, but also prepares you to step into someone else's experience and help that person see God's movement. Perhaps as you are reading right now, you are also thinking of people you want face time with. Take the first step, the first risk, in making it happen and finding an authentic relationship both with God and another person.

## DON'T HARDEN YOUR HEART.

Psalm 95 says, "If only you would listen to his voice today! The LORD says, 'Don't harden your hearts as Israel did'" (95:8). The same theme echoes in the New Testament book of Hebrews (3:7–8, 15; 4:7). And of course, it originated back when Moses was attempting to lead a stubborn bunch of fraidy cats out of bondage and into the Promised Land. I think we rebel against God with our pretending. We harden our hearts when, over and over, we have the opportunity to stop pretending, but we don't. We're afraid of letting go of our comfort zone. We're afraid of losing the control we've worked so hard for. We're afraid of getting close to someone and letting the person know we don't have it together after all.

That sounds like Satan's lies. He tries to get us to buy into the "better just hang on" philosophy instead of really allowing God to have his way. It's hard work to stop pretending, especially if we've built a public image on a pretend foundation.

Life is a progression of seasons. Sometimes we stay in a mode too long—like a forty-something mom trying to wear jeans designed for a teenager who decided not to eat for the last two days. Not cool. But we can convince ourselves of anything if we surround ourselves with people who want to wear that same thing, whether they're built for it or not. Being like everyone else is a comfort zone of its own.

But what if God says, "No, I want you to *wear* something else"? The apostle Paul tells us:

> *Since God chose you to be the holy people he loves, you must clothe yourselves with tenderhearted mercy, kindness, humility, gentleness, and patience. Make allowance for each other's faults and forgive anyone who offends you. Remember, the Lord forgave you, so you must forgive others. Above all, clothe yourselves with love, which binds us all together in perfect harmony.* (Colossians 3:12–14)

That sounds pretty relational to me. It sounds like authentic relationships based on truth and love. It doesn't sound like pretending or going through the motions of being nice.

Don't be afraid of the friend you could become.

## 12

# STRIPPING THE GRAVE CLOTHES

*Being real means you can see past the pain.*

Life is short, so don't fake it." Circle of Friends Ministries invites women to exchange the familiar for the extraordinary. If we risk letting go of protecting ourselves by pretending, we get a chance to find out what God will do in our lives.

We need to admit we are "dead" sometimes. Life can wound us deeply. Even when everything looks great on the outside—as far as anyone else can see—we can be dying on the inside. We show the world our accomplishments or how well we're keeping up with ordinary life, but we know where the pain is. Life is messy. Relationships disintegrate. Illness and accidents happen. If that next paycheck doesn't come, everything will fall apart. Family dynamics stretch us thin. The boss at work is clueless. Parenting is so much harder than we ever imagined. One mistake changes everything.

The mess is there. You know it, and I know it. How do we respond to it? We bury ourselves in busyness with our children. We take on more work than we can possibly handle and still have a healthy life. We watch too much television or crawl around on the Internet until two in the morning. We eat—or we don't eat. We drink. We redecorate. We shop. Or we just ignore the mess and focus on doing the next thing that needs doing until the moment comes to say, "Finally, this day is over."

What will it take for us to show our pain to each other?

## DEATH DOES NOT WIN.

Jesus is not afraid of what others assume is a stinky mess. In John 11 we read the story of the death of his good friend Lazarus and the response of Jesus that surprises everyone.

Mary and Martha, sisters of Lazarus, sent word to Jesus that their brother was sick. I can only imagine they expected him to interrupt his own plans and head for Bethany, where they live. Jesus loved Lazarus, after all, and if anyone could help Lazarus it would be Jesus.

But Jesus stayed put for the next two days. And when he decided to go, his closest followers thought he had lost his marbles. Bethany was in the area where, just a few days earlier, Jewish leaders had been intent on killing Jesus. Why would he go back there?

By this time, Lazarus was dead, and Jesus knew he still had a day's travel ahead of him. He told his friends, "Lazarus is dead. And for your sake, I am glad I wasn't there, for now you will really believe" (John 11:14–15).

Death is not an equal foe of Jesus. In fact, Jesus used the death of Lazarus for God's purpose. It was an opportunity for people to see God's power and believe in him.

When Jesus approached Bethany, he learned that Lazarus had been in the grave four days. Lazarus must have died around the time the messengers first came to tell Jesus he was ill. Lazarus was gone—well beyond any hope of a sudden rally and recovery.

Martha and Mary each said, "Lord, if you had been here, my brother would not have died." To the sisters, Lazarus's death was defeat. They fought death and lost. Their only hope—Jesus—didn't show up in time.

Jesus said, "I am the resurrection and the life. Anyone who believes in me will live, even after dying. Everyone who lives in me and believes in me will never die. Do you believe this, Martha?" (John 11:25–26). Often we quote these verses but leave off the key question: Do you believe?

Martha had her moment of belief and said, "I have always believed you are the Messiah, the Son of God" (John 11:27). Mary's moment followed soon. The grieving crowd had gathered, and Jesus joined them with his own tears. Even though he knew God's purpose in this situation, Jesus was not oblivious to the pain others felt, nor his own. He didn't hesitate to show his own emotion over the death of his friend and the destruction that sin brought on the rebellious earth.

The grave was a cave with a large stone across the entrance. Jesus gave the order to move the stone. Martha—who only moments earlier expressed faith in Jesus—said, "Lord, he has been dead four days. The smell will be terrible" (John 11:39). That didn't stop Jesus. The stone was rolled away, and Jesus called out, "Lazarus, come out!"

And Lazarus came out. He was bound in the grave clothes that marked his death. Even his face was wrapped in a cloth. But he was alive.

## SEE THE GLORY.

Jesus is the one who resurrects. That's his job. So often we fight against letting things die. But when a situation is so full of illness and dysfunction, an element of death is essential before there can be resurrection. In those challenging times we really do have to trust that God's timing is perfect—not four days late—and that his ways are not ours.

When we are in relationship with Jesus, death has a different meaning. "For to me, living means living for Christ, and dying is even better," the apostle Paul wrote in Philippians 1:21. The death of our perspective is what gives way to the resurrection power of God.

"If you had been there," Mary and Martha said. Jesus intentionally waited. From a human perspective, it seems almost cruel. But Jesus saw the whole scenario. He had his eye on a display of the glory of God. Even in our apprehension, embracing God's sovereignty can be such a comfort. When we trust Jesus, we trust he is doing God's work in us. Jesus' work was to obey the will of the Father and show the Father to us. What he shows in this story of the death of Lazarus is that God has a plan. Yes, it does involve suffering, but on the other side of suffering is God's grace at work.

While everybody was freaking out and expecting a stinking mess, Jesus transformed a dire circumstance. When Lazarus came out, he was wrapped in grave clothes, but he was alive. He was raised and transformed to life by Jesus, but Jesus was not the one who walked over to Lazarus and took off the clothes. Jesus said to those who saw the miracle, "Unwrap him and let him go!" (John 11:44). He gave the unwrapping job to Lazarus's friends and family.

That's our part in the miracle. Jesus is the one who saves, but he shares with us the privilege of unwrapping the grave clothes. Lazarus is alive, but he is bound up by what death had brought. The people who care about him help him unwrap and walk free of the signs of death. His friends loosen the bindings. The people who unwrap Lazarus have the privilege of seeing him alive and healthy.

Why do we want to walk around in grave clothes when we're not dead anymore?

The model Jesus gives through the story of Lazarus is for us as well. We need each other to help unwrap the grave clothes. Jesus calls us by name back from death and shows God's glory through our lives. Then he sends us to help each other peel off the signs of death. We have the privilege of being part of God's work of transformation in each other's lives.

Rather than avoid pain at all costs—even though going through it would lead to health—you can face the pain in your life. Hear Jesus calling your name. When you answer his call, a circle of friends can help you peel off the grave clothes.

Resurrection begins in death. Let your pretending die. Exchange the familiar for the extraordinary. Take the risk.

# Love Me Back to Life

I'm falling to pieces,
Pulled under by blame,
Feel like I'm drowning
In an ocean of pain.

I've been imprisoned,
By the walls that I've built,
Caught in the middle
Of time standing still.

Jesus, I need You to hold me,
I'm all alone, it's dark and cold.
Will You come by my side?
Jesus, I need You to hold me.
And love me back to life.

It's hard to lift my head when
I'm covered in despair.
The ugly lies inside me
Are more than I can bear.

I can't imagine
Or see beyond the pain,
When I'm so overwhelmed by
The guilt and the shame.

My dear friend Dawn Yoder wrote this song, which our mutual friend Paul Marino helped fashion into a finished work. She called it "Love Me Back to Life," which is also the title of a novel by Missy Horsfall and Susan Stevens, two other women in our circle of friends. This song describes the work of Jesus in loving us back to life.

—Dawn Yoder/Paul Marino
© 2010 McKinney Music/BMI and Van Ness Press/
ASCAP (admin. by Lifeway Worship)

# Reflections

🐚 How do the words of this song connect with your life?

🐚 What lies does Satan tell you about your life? What's the truth?

🐚 Are you on speaking terms with God? Describe your relationship with God honestly.

🐚 What difficulties do you have with trusting others? With trusting God? If possible, explain what you think the root of the problem is.

🐚 What scars in your life are evidence of healed wounds—physically, emotionally, and spiritually?

🐚 How do you respond to the challenge "Don't be afraid of the friend you could become."

# AFFIRMATION

We dare you to enrich the lives of those around you.
No one else is you.

# 13

# NOT SO HARD

*God moves in our lives and invites us into the lives of others.*

Turning toward authenticity takes guts. If you follow through, your life will never be the same again. Being real with God opens you up to a new kind of living, and being real with other people allows you to enter their lives. Now you journey together in the light rather than alone in shadows.

"What do I have to offer anyone else?" you may be asking.

Plenty.

God created you and gifted you. No one else is you. One of our goals at Circle of Friends is to encourage women in their gifts.

Music.

Writing.

Speaking.

Presenting.

Compassion.

Hospitality.

Friendship.

Picking just the right paint color.

Remembering who is allergic to walnuts.

Singing into your hairbrush without embarrassment.

Using humor to make people feel comfortable.

We can't possibly make a complete list of the gifts and talents people have, but we are committed to affirming the gifts as we see them and offering opportunities for people to do what God calls them to do. We spend too much time secretly ranking gifts in other women, and perhaps being jealous, and too little time discovering and affirming the incredible variety of God's gifts to his people. The Bible is full of stories about women who seemed to have nothing to offer, but we remember them for stepping up in the moment and using the gifts God gave them.

## TASTE AND SEE THAT THE LORD IS GOOD.

Do we make life and ministry too hard? I pondered this question with a friend over a cup of coffee. She had encountered a shift in her ministry responsibility, and I believed that her ability to think creatively and scripturally put her in a position to be a catalyst for fresh growth in areas where her leadership style would flourish.

As we talked, imagery from my background in the food industry flowed into the conversation. I've worked in the food business in some capacity for most of my life. I grew up with it. Some theories apply in both business and ministry.

Sometimes we need to allow a "product" to speak for itself. When our company goes to a trade show, we do a great display—colorful, creative, visually appetizing—but all the pretty stuff won't mean a thing if the taste isn't there. I can lead a consumer to the sampling table, but if the product isn't primo, then it's a no-sale.

The Bible tells us to "taste and see that the LORD is good" (Psalm 34:8). Our souls are hungry for the Bread of Life. When you taste something that you're longing for, you have one of those "That's it!" moments. No matter what you eat after that, you will never satisfy that particular craving apart from an authentic recipe. When you reach out with your gifts to people around you—in your family, in your community—you offer them the chance to taste and see that the Lord is good.

Folks don't gravitate toward stale food. Fresh food can come in either a traditional family recipe or an innovative approach to serving food, but if food has been sitting out on the counter all day or has been in the fridge long enough to start turning colors, it loses its appeal. The tastiest and most nourishing food is fresh, not stale. As you use your gifts to touch the lives of other people, remember to keep your own relationship with God fresh. Grow some new stuff in your spiritual garden, and out of that abundance you will have something to offer so people can taste and see that the Lord is good.

Some of the most enjoyable eating experiences for me come when I am connecting with another person. It might be a romantic dinner with Bob, or laughing and communicating with my accountability group. It might be a meal of comfort after a funeral or a quick bite with my kids. Nourishment in both the physical and spiritual sense is strongly connected to relationships.

## STEP INTO YOUR GIFTS.

When I have the privilege of teaching a small group or meeting with a woman one-on-one, I ask people to tell me about themselves. Even shy people will usually give a glimpse of what is in their hearts. I ask the Lord to help me relate what they are saying to a character in his Word. People identify with other people. If you are talking to someone whose heart is in pieces because of an affair, talk about King David. If someone is wondering when God's going to do what they believe he said he would do,

> I found a place where I am loved for who I am, where I can be real and vulnerable. A place where I am encouraged, inspired, and motivated to be all that God calls me to be, and a place to be blessed and to bless others with my giftings. I found a place of support in the tough times, hands to hold, and shoulders to cry on. I found a circle of true heart friends who are eager to share in the laughter and tears. —Dayna

talk about Abraham and Sarah. If someone is falsely accused of inappropriate actions and their reputation destroyed, talk about Joseph.

Contextual simplicity is the art of humbly allowing God to work through his Word, his Spirit, and your submissive heart to present truth to a seeking soul. Spending time in God's Word is essential preparation. God speaks great volumes in a still, small voice, but when we hide his Word in our hearts, we have the tools to discern what his Spirit says. If you have a hard time grasping concepts you encounter in the Bible, ask someone who is further along in the Christian journey to teach you.

For the next several chapters of this book, I invite you to step into some powerful passages from the Bible—stories of women on their own journeys with God. Let yourself see what they see and feel what they feel. Then watch as they grab hold of the gifts God put at their disposal in some pretty outlandish ways. Because they answered God's call, the lives around them were changed. Let them be an example to you as you step into your own gifts.

# 14

# The Truth about
# the Proverbs 31 Wife

*Measure against the right standard.*

"Who can find a virtuous and capable wife? She is more precious than rubies" (Proverbs 31:10).

Are you squirming yet?

If you're a wife, Proverbs 31 might not be one of your favorite passages of the Bible. It certainly sets the standard high. Even if you're not a wife right now, this passage puts a lot of eggs in the basket of being a good one.

The woman described in the closing verses of Proverbs cooks before dawn, puts food on the table, shops with savvy, spins her own cloth and sews warm clothes for her family, wheels and deals in real estate, runs the farm, takes care of the poor, quilts her own bedding, cheerfully looks forward to the future, and generally all around makes her husband proud by doing everything with excellence.

Whew.

It's enough to make most of us say, "Well, sure, I could do all that if I were rich and had a house full of servants."

Sometimes we reduce the whole chapter down to that one sentiment. "Whoever this woman is," we say, "she doesn't live in my universe."

## LISTEN TO THE QUEEN MOTHER'S ADVICE.

Proverbs 31:10–31 is a form of poetry, an acrostic. The passage was written in Hebrew, so the first word of each line begins with the next letter of the Hebrew alphabet. That means the author has to come up with twenty-two reasons to extol this extraordinary woman. In the process, the writer seems determined not to leave out even the smallest activity of this model wife.

What happens if we back up a bit and get a running start at these verses? Let's go back to the beginning of the chapter. "The sayings of King Lemuel contain this message, which his mother taught him" (Proverbs 31:1). Before the section describing an excellent wife comes some advice from the king's mother herself.

Lemuel was not a king of Israel. We don't really know who he is or how his writings got attached to the end of Proverbs. But let's not get lost in that mystery and lose sight of the fact that this advice comes from his mother. She doesn't mince words. Her warnings in the first nine verses of the chapter are about wine and women. She knows well the weak points where powerful men fall under attack, on the one hand, and the responsibilities of the king on the other. "Rulers should not crave alcohol," she says. "For if they drink, they may forget the law and not give justice to the oppressed" (Proverbs 31:4–5). "Speak up for those who cannot speak for themselves," she reminds her son. "Ensure justice for those being crushed. Yes, speak up for the poor and helpless, and see that they get justice" (Proverbs 31:8–9).

The king's mother tells him to be just and to be a protector and provider, before she describes the virtuous woman. His responsibilities as a leader and a husband are front and center. If the king does what the wise woman who raised him tells him to do, he will turn out to be a decent person who takes his responsibility seriously. He will live not in a way that feeds his own pleasures. Instead, he will show God's priorities for justice and care of the poor.

## IS IT POETRY AND PRACTICALITIES?

This is the set-up for the poetic passage about the ideal wife. What mom wouldn't want her son to marry someone who is virtuous and capable? It's common sense. The husband of the Proverbs 31 wife can trust her. She enriches his life. Rather than being a hindrance that drags him down, she is a help.

I know what it's like to feel like a hindrance. I felt as if I failed my husband because of my ongoing struggles with depression. I thought I was abnormal, and that I pulled Bob down. My depression certainly was a challenge, but it was one that we could address. Unfortunately, too many people still attach a stigma to mental health issues, even depression, which is more common than you think. Even from pulpits I hear people implying that if you suffer from depression you don't have victory in Jesus. Would anyone say that about diabetes or heart disease? Depression, or another mental health issue, is not in a separate, less spiritual category than other physical illness. I would love to be healed. I've even had people lay hands on me and pray for healing. We want women and men to be capable and enrich the lives of their spouses and families. When a physical hindrance gets in the way, we should not make anyone feel of less value. Am I virtuous and capable—despite my history of depression? Yes, I am. My virtue comes from believing what God says about me.

Nobody's perfect. We all have our reasons for feeling like a hindrance to other people. You might not be depressed, but perhaps you are painfully shy, or nonathletic, or craft-impaired, or can't bake your way out of a paper bag. I don't have to tell you what it's like to be in a situation where you don't quite feel like you're keeping up or fitting in. It's so easy to settle our minds on what we're *not* good at that we fail to accept and affirm what we *are* good at.

Who can possibly achieve what this woman in Proverbs 31 manages to do? We could work our whole lives and not accomplish what she seems to get done on a daily basis.

*She finds wool and flax and busily spins it. She is like a merchant's ship, bringing her food from afar. She gets up before dawn to prepare breakfast for her household and plan the day's work for her servant girls. She goes out to inspect a field and buys it; with her earnings she plants a vineyard. She is energetic and strong, a hard worker. She makes sure her dealings are profitable; her lamp burns late into the night.*

*Her hands are busy spinning thread, her fingers twisting fiber. She extends a helping hand to the poor and opens her arms to the needy.*

*She has no fear of winter for her household for everyone has warm clothes. She makes her own bedspreads. She dresses in fine linen and purple gowns.* (Proverbs 31:13–22)

She certainly is industrious and accomplished—intimidating, even—is there anything she can't do? Talk about feeling like we fall short!

Notice the blend of tasks that are traditionally women's work and endeavors that are not. The ideal woman in the Bible is not servile and domestic. She's not turning away from her talents in order to be a more acceptable wife. She's actually putting them to use, and she happens to be pretty good at business.

On the domestic side, I particularly like the line telling us she plans the day for her servant girls. More than one! Perhaps a nanny, an upstairs maid, and a downstairs maid. Wouldn't that be the life?

Let's not get too caught up in the daydream. What that little line really tells us is that this woman doesn't have to do it all. She accepts help.

I'm not good at everything. People in my life will be much better off if I love them and spend time with them and allow someone else to take care of the tasks they're better at doing. My friend Beth is good at keeping financial books, so why would I want to be the treasurer of Circle of Friends? Why would I sew something for my kids when it would not look good or wear well? Too many women feel that they have to do everything themselves or

> *Circle of Friends has given me a support system I never experienced before. Through Christ's love, they share my burdens with me during times of despair. With Jesus as the focus of our relationships, we have been able to love one another on a deep level that cannot be found elsewhere. I realize that the love we have for one another is driven by the power of the Holy Spirit. I owe so much of my sanity to the lovely ladies of this ministry. —Caroline*

else they're not good wives and mothers. Add a job and ministry into the mix, and the challenge is overwhelming.

I don't have to do it all either. Neither do you. Part of understanding and affirming each other's gifts is recognizing where one ends and another begins.

## YOUR GIFTS ENRICH OTHERS.

Unquestionably, the Proverbs 31 woman is busy. She sets the bar high. But the standard is not so much the quantity and variety of work she accomplishes as it is the character at the core of her life. She has true character—clothed in strength and dignity, with no fear of the future. She speaks wisely and with kindness. Her children think she's terrific, and her husband boasts about her. Try on a different pair of glasses and read the passage looking for indications of this woman's character, rather than her skill in running a household.

She brings the blessings of God to her family (vv. 10–12, 23, 28).

She works hard and does not take the easy way out (vv. 15, 17).

She is resourceful (vv. 18, 24).

She is generous to the poor (v. 20).

She has a positive attitude (v. 25).

She brings dignity to everything she does (v. 25).

She chooses her words carefully (v. 26).

Verse 30 sums it all up: "Charm is deceptive, and beauty does not last; but a woman who fears the LORD will be greatly praised." All the things we try to be good at fall under the charm and beauty umbrella. We try to impress people—and perhaps ourselves—by being good at the right things and presenting our lives tied up in pretty bows for others to admire. But that's not really what Proverbs 31 is about.

This woman shows us what wisdom looks like in the life of someone living it in her daily routine. If we get too hung up on the list of accomplishments, we miss the picture of her character. Without this character, rooted in a deep respect and love for God, even this woman with all her talents would be nothing.

Offering care and nurturing to those whom God gives you, as the woman in Proverbs 31 does, shows God's love. As a wife, I always want to bring physical, emotional, and spiritual pleasure to my husband. He deserves nothing less. I don't get it right all the time, but my motive is to love Bob well. I am blessed to be a mom, and I have a responsibility to be the best mom I can be. When I'm unsure, I can ask for help. Both my mom and my mother-in-law balanced caretaking within the home with serving those outside the family. They understood the value of delegating tasks so that everyone benefited. That's wisdom. The woman in Proverbs 31 understands this.

Can you run an import business and handle the legalities of property transactions? Can you spin your own cloth and sew your own clothes? Perhaps not. But you can love God. You can be generous and positive and kind. Learn from this woman's character and let God show you how the gifts he gives you enrich the lives of others.

# 15

# TAMAR'S LET-DOWN

*You can find significance even if your life is sordid.*

Tamar had to find a way to survive, making her not so different from a lot of women I know. She trusted the men in her life to do the right thing, and they left her hanging. Sound familiar? In spite of a rather sordid life story, Tamar ended up being an ancestor of Jesus, the Savior of the world.

Let's start with some background to Tamar's story. God promised a son to Abraham and Sarah, and they waited twenty-five years for God to keep his promise. After that slow start, things picked up. Isaac, their son, grew up. Abraham did not want Isaac to marry a foreigner, so he sends an entourage to find him a bride from their own extended family. Enter Rebekah. Isaac and Rebekah had two sons, Jacob and Esau. Jacob had twelve sons. God's promise to Abraham included too many descendants to count. We're starting to see how that was going to happen.

One of Jacob's sons was Judah, and he married a Canaanite woman. Perhaps he went against his father's wishes in marrying a foreigner. Judah and his bride birthed three little boys in quick succession: Er, Onan, and Shelah.

The boys grew up, and now it was time to find a bride for the oldest boy, Er. Judah arranged a marriage between Er and Tamar, who was probably another foreigner. But Er was wicked—we don't know what his sin was— and God took his life before the newlyweds had any children. It wasn't Tamar's fault that Er died. He was the one who had sinned, not her. But now her future dangled.

The right thing was for Judah to give Tamar to his next son, Onan. The first male child they had would be Er's legal heir. So Judah did this. Onan married Tamar and seemed to have no problem with the marriage—but he was not having a baby for his brother. He had his limits. So he denied her the opportunity to conceive. Tamar, the outsider, was just trying to do the right thing, including fulfilling the promise to Abraham for more descendants than he could count. Ironically, Onan, the great-grandson of Abraham, deliberately works against God's promise.

The writer of Genesis tells us, "The LORD considered it evil for Onan to deny a child to his dead brother. So the LORD took Onan's life, too" (Genesis 38:10).

So where did that leave Tamar? She did the right thing by one husband. He died. She did the right thing by a second man, and he died. Now she was depending on her father-in-law to do the right thing again.

Judah decided his third son, Shelah, was too young for marriage. So he suggested Tamar go back to her parents' house while everybody waited for Shelah to grow up a little more. Technically, Tamar was engaged to marry Shelah, but the wedding plans were in limbo. That was the official position. The truth was Judah had no intention of marrying off another son to Tamar. Two sons already died after marrying this woman. He was not taking any chances with his last son.

Judah's wife died. After an appropriate period of time, his eyes started to wander in the female direction. Judah and his buddy Hirah went to a village called Timnah for the busy sheep-shearing time. Tamar got wind of the trip and saw her chance. Enough time had passed that Shelah was plenty

---

*I confided in a couple of my new circle of friends about my past, and they have been soothing and welcoming. They affirm me in my new Christ-centered life. They don't judge.. They support and uplift me and help by listening when I struggle. They want me to grow in my walk and get closer to God every day. They help me to see I am beautiful when I see myself through the eyes of God. They encourage me even when it is simply something I hear through the radio. They have no idea how their words affect listeners every day. —Millie*

old enough to get married, so why hadn't Judah sent for her? Up until now, Tamar had been fairly passive, playing by the rules in a man's world. But in the face of injustice, she found her spine. Judah owed her a son!

Tamar disguised herself and headed out to the road on the way to Timnah. Judah came along, assumed she was a prostitute, and made an offer.

This was Tamar's moment. Judah wanted her. She didn't waste the chance to ask for something big. Judah promised a nice juicy goat, but she wanted some collateral—his identification seal, cord, and walking stick. Judah would agree to anything to have his way with her and handed over these items that carried serious legal weight.

Later, when Judah wanted to deliver the goat and get his stuff back, he sent his friend Hirah. The problem was, Hirah couldn't find the woman anywhere. In fact, everybody in the village denied they even had a prostitute in their sweet town. Judah could have been in for some deep embarrassment if he pushed the issue further, so he resigned himself to the fact that this strange, unknown woman would keep his things.

Tamar got pregnant—so far so good for her plan. Word got back to Judah, and it was a problem for him. This woman was technically engaged to his son Shelah. What business did she have being with another man? And rumors that her predicament was a result of prostitution made things worse. Judah couldn't ignore this offense. "Bring her out, and let her be burned!" Judah shouted (Genesis 38:24).

At this most strategic moment, Tamar produces Judah's things, saying, "The man who owns this identification seal and walking stick is the father of my child. Do you recognize them?"

Judah messed up when he didn't give his third son to Tamar.

Judah messed up when he approached a woman he thought was a prostitute.

But now Judah was ready to do the right thing. "She is more in the right than I am," he said publicly. A few months later, Tamar gave birth to twin sons. One of them, Perez, became an ancestor of David, Israel's greatest king. Without Tamar's determination to have a son, Judah would not have been in the family line that led to Jesus.

## "Sordid" and "significant" are not mutually exclusive.

Tamar is not so different from a lot of women. Tough situations exist all around us. I know women who feel as desperate as Tamar did, and you probably know some too. Her choice to seduce Judah to get what she wanted might give us the shivers, but let's not miss her motivation.

Tamar wanted a child who would be part of the promise to Abraham, the people of God. She wanted justice. She wanted the men she depended on to do the right thing.

As a society, we're in no position to be self-righteous about what Tamar did. A woman I know is engaged, and her fiancé's half brother is the former boyfriend of his mother. A dad seduces his son's girlfriend. A woman sleeps with her husband's son. Inappropriate relationships are all around us, and I don't just mean on television or at the movies. We live in a sinful, broken society. Real people find themselves in these situations. You can probably name some of them.

How do we respond? That's the question.

Do we judge? Do we distance ourselves from the messiness? Do we shake our heads at the notion that anyone could do such a morally depraved deed?

Brokenness leads to children without parents, parents without partners, and people whom God loves living without hope. More and more we seem happy to let social services take on responsibilities for broken lives. Government programs spend our tax dollars on social services, or we donate to a fund-raiser for a nonprofit group whose mission is to care for the people who live on the margins of our society. I often wonder what could happen if more Christians embraced a sense of responsibility to care for people with a personal touch.

Tamar believed in God's promise to Abraham to raise up a people, and she wanted to be part of the promise. Tamar had determination, resourcefulness, and smarts. She put them all to work to climb out of an unjust, despairing situation. She found significance, and we remember her as an ancestor of Jesus.

Tamar's story gives us hope. Perhaps other people have disappointed you and left you stranded physically, emotionally, or financially. Perhaps you've made some questionable decisions out of a noble motive. When you feel caught in the circumstances of your own life, and everything is not going as well as you'd like, remember Tamar. She discovered her own gifts and found her place in God's plan.

The end of the story is that God redeemed the situation. As sordid as Tamar's life was, God welcomed her into his family and made her part of his promise to send a Savior. Her name appears in Matthew's genealogy of Jesus. Tamar was not beyond God's redemption, and neither are you. No matter what your circumstances, God can make something significant and beautiful out of your life.

# 16

# Jael's Judgment

*Your ministry might come right to you.*

By the time of the early chapters of the Old Testament book of Judges, Israel had grown into a nation. Jacob's twelve sons spawned twelve tribes that came out of slavery in Egypt and conquered the land God promised to give Abraham hundreds of years earlier. But the people didn't always listen to God, and they found themselves in repeating cycles where God allowed a foreign king to misdirect his people for a generation or so and then raise up a deliverer to clean up the mess.

In Judges 4, that deliverer was supposed to be a military officer by the name of Barak. Deborah, judge and prophet of Israel at the time, announced that God had called Barak to deliver the nation from the foreign king Jabin of Hazor. God said to Barak, "I will call out Sisera, commander of Jabin's army, along with his chariots and warriors, to the Kishon River. There I will give you victory over him" (Judges 4:7).

Barak hesitated. He'd only answer the call if Deborah went with him into battle. What's with that? Because of this, Deborah said God would use a woman to do the job instead. To a man of Barak's accomplishments, this was a slap in the face. At first glance, we might think that Deborah herself was the woman of the hour, but let's not jump to conclusions and miss God's surprise.

Deborah went into gear and mobilized Barak and ten thousand other soldiers to face the great Sisera. The fact that Sisera had nine hundred chariots would suggest he expected victory, but things didn't go his way. With his chariots stuck in the mud, Sisera found himself running for his life on foot. He arrived at the tent of Jael. She was a nobody, a woman in a nomadic culture who was subject to the whims of her husband. Most likely she never wandered too far from wherever her husband told her to pitch he tent.

Jael's husband was on friendly terms with Jabin, so Sisera no doubt expected a warm reception. But Jael remembered that her people, the Kenites, were long-lost relatives of Moses, the leader who took the Israelites out of slavery in Egypt. Jael didn't do what anyone expected her to do. She decided to throw in her lot with the God of Israel. Instead of protecting Sisera, she lures him into a trap. "Come into my tent, sir. Come in. Don't be afraid" (Judges 4:18). She covered the exhausted warrior with a blanket, and when he asked for water, she went one step better and offered him a glass of milk. Perhaps she was already thinking about what would make him feel both trusting and sleepy. He gave the order for her to stand guard at the tent door and lie to anyone who came looking for him.

Instead, Jael crept up to the sleeping man and hammered a tent peg through his head.

We visualize the gruesome deed and think Jael's actions amounted to horrendous violence. But that's not the main point. Jael's true bravery was in seizing the moment she didn't know was coming when she got up that morning and went out to milk the goats.

## YOUR MINISTRY MAY BE ON YOUR DOORSTEP.

Jael did not have anything to do with the decision to go into battle. None of the circumstances of army fighting army were her doing. Most likely, the outcome of the battle between Barak of Israel and Sisera of Canaan would not change her life, so we might say she didn't even have a dog in the fight. Perhaps she was looking for news of the battle when she went out to the road to meet Sisera, or perhaps she didn't care what happened. Either way, the opportunity to be involved in what God was doing came right to her doorstep, literally, and Jael chose to be part of it.

A lot of things happen all around you that you don't have any ability to influence. Friends encounter trying circumstances, or even tragedy, and you find yourself involved. You may not even be looking to get involved with a cause, but suddenly someone stands on your doorstep and needs your help.

We don't know a lot about Jael, but we know she was somebody's wife, so perhaps she was also a mother. We know she was at home in the middle of the day. We know she was not a famous leader or celebrity. That was Deborah, the mover-and-shaker, high profile leader known all over Israel and around the region. But Jael was a low-profile nomadic wife who spent her days keeping the household running. We can easily imagine that she felt her plate was full just looking after her family and minding her own business.

And that is exactly the person God chose. He didn't pull her away from her family and send her into a leadership training program. He didn't hand her a manual to master some new skill she might need someday. He didn't even tell her to go down the road and find out what the neighbors were up to over in the next camp.

God brought the opportunity right to Jael, a stay-at-home mom. Sisera thought Jael was harmless and could not imagine she posed any threat to anyone, but God had other plans.

I wonder if Satan sees us as harmless sometimes. The Jaels among us are busy wives and moms running errands and driving carpools and changing diapers. We're looking after our own homes and families. Maybe your husband, like Jael's, has made a more convenient alliance than doing what God asks. When he goes golfing on Sunday morning, you pack up the kids and go to church alone. What threat are we? Satan thinks the little religious

*This wonderful circle of friends came around me as I was going through a horribly dark time. I began listening to them on the radio and immediately felt accepted and loved, even though I had never met them. They spoke God's words to my ears. I went to one of their conferences during a snowstorm—I would not have missed it for anything! There I got to meet my new circle of friends face-to-face, and I knew I had found a place to belong. —Sharon*

mom is harmless because she doesn't often get out into real life. But she's the woman on the cul-de-sac who knows Jesus can make a difference right there. What if God brings the ministry right to your door, just the way he did for Jael?

## BE READY FOR YOUR MOMENT.

Maybe you don't have to leave the cul-de-sac to find the ministry God wants to give you for this season in your life.

We're not Stepford wives, after all. Some of us may be busy with marriage and child rearing and homemaking as a season of life, but we didn't come out of cookie molds. We have pasts, and some of them are painful. Sisera arrived at Jael's door burdened and exhausted from the battle, and Jael had a moment of discernment to understand how his evil was a threat to God's people. You may meet someone today who is burdened and exhausted from the battle of her life, taunted by some memory, running from what persecutes her, and you may have a moment when you can see the evil that threatens this person's life. When a moment of call comes to your doorstep, will you answer?

Jael's hammer and tent peg were the tools of her ordinary life. When a nomadic family reached a new location, the wife's job was to set up the tent. When the moment of call came—an opportunity to step into what God was doing for his people—Jael reached for the tools of her ordinary life. Right where you are, whatever the pieces of your life are right now, God wants to use you. Don't try to limit God by thinking you're not a leader or don't have special talent. Jael's story shows us that God uses common people right in the context of their everyday lives. God calls ordinary people, however unlikely, to do extraordinary things in his kingdom.

God wants to use you. Will you answer his call when it turns up on your doorstep? Can you be trusted with the tools God gives you to slay the lies and deceptions Satan uses to attack the heart of a neighbor?

# 17

# LYDIA THE BUSINESSWOMAN

*Your talents open doors to ministry.*

What do we know about Lydia?
She lived in Philippi.
She was not Jewish, but she worshipped God.
She met with a circle of friends along the river for prayer.
She was a businesswoman.
She was likely wealthy.
She was hungry to learn about Jesus.
She was persistent.
She opened her home and perhaps started a church.

Lydia's story is covered in just a few verses in the New Testament book of Acts. Paul was on one of several major evangelistic journeys recorded in Acts. Traveling with Silas and Luke, he arrived in Philippi, a major city of the district of Macedonia and a Roman colony. Paul's usual habit upon arriving in a new place was to seek out the Jews first and tell them the good news of Jesus the Messiah. Then he would move on to the Gentiles. However, Philippi had no Jewish synagogue because the city had so few Jews—not even the ten married men required to begin a synagogue. Instead, a small group met along the river to pray on the Sabbath. So Paul headed for the river and sat down with a group of women.

Lydia was there.

*One of them was Lydia from Thyatira, a merchant of expensive purple cloth, who worshipped God. As she listened to us, the Lord opened her heart, and she accepted what Paul was saying. She was baptized along with other members of her household, and she asked us to be her guests. "If you agree that I am a true believer in the Lord," she said, "come and stay at my home." And she urged us until we agreed.* (Acts 16:14–15)

Purple cloth was expensive. Regular people didn't wear purple, because it was a sign of royalty or belonging to the upper class, and it cost a pretty penny. So if Lydia was a merchant of purple cloth, then she was running a high-end business for wealthy clients and most likely did pretty well for herself as a result.

But Lydia was not carried away by her own success. She was seeking God. She worshipped God. She prayed to God. Lydia was not a full-fledged convert to the Jewish religion, but she knew that the Jews had the one true God. So her heart was ripe for Paul's message. Perhaps this women's prayer group did not often have a teacher with them. Lydia ate up everything Paul had to say. The Lord moved in her heart and gave her faith to believe the truth. Her faith impacted her whole household, and she and at least some of her loved ones chose to be baptized.

Lydia want Paul and his entourage to be her personal guests at her home. Perhaps they hesitated for some reason, but Lydia had her mind made up. Luke, the writer of Acts, says, "She urged us until we agreed."

This chapter in Acts goes on to tell the more famous story of Paul and Silas getting arrested and locked up in chains in prison for preaching the gospel. After a miraculous release, where did they go? Back to Lydia's house (Acts 16:40), where they met with other believers to encourage them. Lydia's home had become "believer's central" in Philippi. A prominent businesswoman was now determined to transform her community.

## YOUR MINISTRY MAY BE ON THE JOB.

I can relate to Lydia. So many women work, and sometimes because of being involved in the corporate world, we wonder where ministry fits in. I believe—and have seen for myself—that God provides for his work through the gifts and talents of those who do well in their vocations. He gives the heart of generosity and leadership to be able to see what he is doing and to become part of God's work through sharing resources. When I look at Lydia, I see her generous spirit. Paul's ministry touched her life, and she immediately wanted to be part of sharing the gospel. I imagine she was a welcome blessing to Paul's ministry. In the circles she ran in, the story of her conversion no doubt impacted those she did business with—at least to make them curious about the gospel. Lydia could have stayed home and prayed, but she made time in her busy schedule for the social and relational aspects of her spiritual life. She went to the river to meet with others, and the day changed her life. As a result, she could touch the lives of the people around her.

How much of an influence are we where we work? Do people look at us as someone like Lydia—seeking after God, ready and eager to share in his work?

Years ago I met Anya through my business circles. A Russian Jewish woman from Brooklyn, Anya was born in the Ukraine and came to New York with her family as a teenager. Anya is an accomplished person, once named as Jewish Businesswoman of the Year in a major city in the eastern United States, and a leader in a national Jewish charitable organization. She is one of the smartest, most assertive women I've ever met. Very wealthy, very beautiful, very powerful. Yet she's still searching for meaning.

Originally Anya contacted me because our family business had a product she wanted. Her specialty niche is supplying Russian populations in North America, and she believed one of our products would fit well in her system. I had been dealing with other Russian distributors at the time, all men with foul language and determined to barter with me. I really learned to stand my ground. Anya wanted to buy this particular item from us, but I couldn't sell it to her. We had an exclusive agreement with another distributor in the area. I suggested other items Anya might be interested in, but she was not pleased. Her attitude was *Nobody tells me no.*

"Why won't you sell me this product?" she demanded to know.

"I'm a Christian," I answered, "and I keep my word. You can buy anything else, but not that."

"Well, what else do you have?" she asked reluctantly.

Anya began to sell other products in the same market as the distributor with the exclusive agreement, and she did well. We went on to develop custom products together to complement her existing line without compromising my agreement with the other distributor. Eventually the other distributor sold out to another company, ending the exclusive agreement. Now I was free to sell Anya the product she originally wanted. Business increased even more, and we continued to grow the personal dimension of our relationship in the context of doing business together.

On September 12, 2001, Anya called me.

"Okay, Lisa," she said, "you know God. Why did this happen?"

This was the question on so many people's minds. The entire country was devastated the day before by the terrorist attacks that took down the World Trade Center in New York. Anya heard the first plane from her office and stood on the roof of her building and watched the second plane's impact.

"Sin," I answered, "that's why. Sin is why Jesus came. We need to be rescued."

God is wooing Anya, and he has invited me to be part of the process. Bob and Jillian have witnessed my tears after conversations with Anya. They know the depth of the burden the Lord has given me for her. I love her. My heavy heart cannot accept the thought of a Christ-less eternity for her. So I keep on. Whenever we get together, I know Anya wants me to come for a business visit but also a personal visit.

"You almost seem like a Zionist," she said to me once.

"I wouldn't have salvation if it were not for the Jews," I answered.

"How do you know that Jesus is Messiah?"

"Because of the writings of Isaiah." From the writings of Isaiah, a Jewish prophet in the Old Testament, I showed Anya God's plan for the suffering servant who would be the Messiah.

It's God's responsibility to save Anya, but my heart is burdened for her. God calls me to show the love of Jesus to Anya, no matter what struggles she shares, and no matter whether I agree with her choices. She is looking for Messiah. Sometimes it might be easier to hit "ignore" on my phone or postpone talking to her, but it seems as though every time I talk with her, I have opportunity to speak into her life as well as conduct business. I continue to practice integrity in my business while also practicing relational evangelism. Others have offered to take the products I sell to Anya and perhaps distribute in greater quantities, which would be good for our business. But if I did that, it could undo what God has invited me to be part of over the years with Anya. God wants to love her through me. Through the venue of the marketplace, we have developed a heart relationship that I pray will endure for eternity, with both of us worshipping the Messiah promised through Abraham, Isaac, and Jacob.

Anya will sometimes call and say, "Better tell your friends to start praying for me," because of some circumstance in her life. She knows that Christian women in the Midwest are praying for her even if she doesn't pray for herself—and when she does pray, she wonders if God is listening to her.

Business is never just business. Someday God is going to ask me for an account of what I did in business, and it won't be about the bottom line. We're a family business, and the people we do business with are an extension of our family. How do I want to treat my family members, and how do I want them to treat me?

## HUNGER FOR GOD.

Lydia did not put the pieces of her life into separate compartments. She was a prominent businessperson, but she was also a woman seeking God, and she didn't try to hide this side of herself. Lydia went to where other God-seekers gathered—and where others could see her and know what she was doing.

Then when Lydia became a Christian through Paul's ministry, she didn't just send a check to support his work while she went about making lots of money and living extravagantly. She opened her own home and put herself at the heartbeat of Christian ministry in the region.

Whatever your work involves, let me challenge you to see it as an opportunity for ministry. Who are the people God brings across your path because of your work? How can you show Christ to other people through the decisions you make at work? How do business deals and relationships come together in your setting?

God gives you particular abilities and unique opportunities that emerge in the way you earn a living. You don't work in a box separate from the rest of your life. I don't care if you run a billion-dollar international company or if you're the lunch lady at the local school. I want to encourage you to see that you can be part of what God is doing wherever you are, whatever your talents.

We don't know a lot about Lydia, but we know she was hungry for God and made a difference. So can you.

# 18

# Your Circle of Friends

*Community enhances your ministry.*

Dawn is an essential part of the music ministry at Circle of Friends. But once upon a time I couldn't have dreamed that she and I would have the friendship God granted us.

Dawn is gifted, intelligent, and godly. Our kids went to the same school. And I didn't think she liked me.

My friend Tammy invited me to an event where the speaker wanted to pray for women in leadership. On guitar, Dawn was part of the team providing music as a context for the prayer time. I felt the Lord nudge me to approach Dawn about playing for a few minutes so Dawn could go be prayed for.

I didn't want to. As I explained to God, I didn't think Dawn liked me.

However, I wanted to be obedient. So I approached Dawn, who was surprised at my suggestion but handed me her guitar and went for prayer. When she returned, I gave the guitar back and invited her to sing on the Circle of Friends worship team. Our annual conference was coming up soon. Dawn has been with Circle of Friends ever since and now is even on our board of directors.

You never know who is going to be in your circle of friends!

## Be open to friends in unsuspecting places.

Ruth owned a business in town. A group of women from Circle of Friends had the opportunity to go to Knoxville, stay together in a cabin, and be part of the support team for the Circle of Friends DVD being produced by my friend and Christian radio and media expert, Linda Meyers. Ruth was part of the group, and we encouraged her to bring a guest. She invited her sister, Grace.

I had a hard time getting a read on Grace while we were recording the program, but I wanted to get to know her better. I don't like to push relationships. God will open the door when the time is right. On the last night in Knoxville, our group sat around and sang and prayed together. Grace was just sitting there. The moment came when I knew how to open a short conversation with Grace.

"What do you like to do?" I asked.

"I love music," she answered.

"Have you ever written a song?"

"I write poetry."

Together we went out to the porch, and a couple of hours later we had the framework of a song.

Grace has a peaceful spirit. She is not someone who puts herself forward. But it turned out she was quite gifted and was thrilled to work together on that song. What a blessing she turned out to be for me! And to think I might never have known her.

My own beloved mother-in-law lost a young adult son to an accident then battled breast cancer, depression, and Parkinson's. When she died, an unreal number of people came to her funeral and told story after story of how Mary touched their lives through Christian Women's Clubs, hosting Bible studies, and connecting her life to the lives of women in the community.

---

*There is no magic formula for a circle of friends. It happens when individuals are willing to be vulnerable, members remain trustworthy, and Christ is the center of each heart. Differences are a good thing, because each difference brings us one step closer to achieving what we might be lacking. Trusting Jesus to fill in the gaps of our personalities, each woman in my circle of friends has brought out the best in me. And after all, isn't that what Jesus does? —Caroline*

On an individual basis, perhaps none of those women glimpsed the bigger picture of Mary's impact on women's ministry in our town. Through Mary's life, and now through her death, they were all connected in a circle of friends.

## I comfort you. You comfort me.

2 Corinthians 1:3–4 has been a "life verse" for me.

*All praise to God, the Father of our Lord Jesus Christ. God is our merciful Father and the source of all comfort. He comforts us in all our troubles so that we can comfort others. When they are troubled, we will be able to give them the same comfort God has given us.*

What we can give to others is in direct correlation to what God has done in our hearts and lives. Whatever road we walk, God is there to comfort us. Out of that comfort, we offer comfort to others on the roads they walk. If we will receive by faith what God's Word tells us, then we will experience the fullness of his love, peace, joy—and a depth of understanding about his character. We show God to each other.

I comfort you. You comfort me.

I tell you the truth. You tell me the truth.

I affirm you. You affirm me.

That's a circle of friends.

Circle of Friends is a ministry that reaches women through music, radio conversation, counseling, conferences, and personal relationships. But our goal is *not* to connect women to our ministry as an end in itself. Our goal is to see women *connected to each other*, comforting *each other* in the realities of their lives and affirming *each other* in using the gifts God gives them.

A circle of friends is not a place to belong for the sake of getting comfortable. Rather, it is a place to belong in order to discover and explore what God means for us to do.

No one else is you.

No one else brings to the table exactly what you bring.

How abundantly you can enrich the lives of the people around you when you take hold of the gifts God gives you and open your heart up to putting them to use.

# Your Love Endures Forever

God of gods, who is like You?
Who can know the depths of Your heart?
Beautiful Savior, of mercy,
You touch me, and I know

Your love endures forever,
Your love endures forever,
It will never change.
Your love remains forever
And ever.

Lamb of God, I adore You.
My hope is here in Your arms.
Beautiful Savior, of mercy,
You heal me, and I know

Your love endures forever,
Your love endures forever,
It will never change.
Your love remains forever
Forever.

Your love endures,
Your love endures,
Your love endures,
Forever.

— Gary Sadler/Susan Ashton/John Hartley/
©2010 Paintbrush Music/ASCAP/Susan Ashton/ASCAP/
Thankyou Music (admin by EMICMGPublishing.com/
ASCAP)

# Reflections

🕯 How do the words of this song connect with your life?

🕯 How does character turn in up in giftedness in your life?

🕯 What circumstances in your life challenge you to reach out in resourceful ways?

🕯 Do you ever get jealous of another woman's gifts? How do you resolve your feelings?

🕯 Who do you identify with most: the woman in Proverbs 31, Tamar, Jael, or Lydia? Why?

🕯 Name three women in your life who would be encouraged to receive affirmation from you of their gifts.

# ACCOUNTABILITY

We encourage you to receive the comfort of companionship.
Be set free!

# 19

# Turning Grief to Joy

*Fear is not the last word.*

At Christmastime in 2006, I drove my aunt Alice to the hospital to see my uncle Don, who had a heart attack. Uncle Don was a good man, but he had not put his faith in Jesus, and Alice was overwhelmed at the thought that he might die before he did. I prayed for him in his hospital bed that day, but both his physical life and his salvation were in God's hands.

Uncle Don recovered, by God's grace. Then on the night of February 17, 2007, he was in an SUV with Alice, their daughter, Kim, and son-in-law, Larry, and three grandsons. In the winter freeze, an empty log truck coming down the hill from the other direction slid into the SUV.

It's the sort of horror you see in the movies but never imagine will happen to people you love.

Aunt Alice died instantly. My cousin's husband, Larry, died instantly. Uncle Don broke his neck but survived. Some of the other injuries were severe as well. My cousin Kim lost her mother and her husband, and three family members were in intensive care.

Talk about a life-changing moment.

One evening, as I was getting ready to sit with my uncle through the night, I first attended a Circle of Friends board meeting. We were days away from our annual conference. The others could have planned the event without me, however. I really stopped by the meeting because I wanted to be with my own circle of friends and ask them to pray for me as I spent the night with my uncle. We prayed specifically that Uncle Don would know Jesus as Lord.

At the hospital, as I settled in, Uncle Don said, "I don't know what I'm going to do without Alice."

"Do you understand that you can see her again?" I asked.

"I want to," he said.

"Do you know the only way that you will?"

"The only way is because of what Jesus Christ has done for me," Uncle Don said.

He was agitated and restless throughout the night, but in that window he was lucid. I heard him say what he believed. One of the most delightful text messages I've ever sent was copying my friends and letting them know what Uncle Don said. They wept with me through my grief, and now they rejoiced with me. Mourning gave way to joy. For those of us left behind, the winds of grief from the day of the accident now blew the joy of resurrection. I can only imagine the joy my aunt Alice must have known from heaven when my uncle spoke of the resurrected Christ.

## GRIEF CAN TURN TO JOY.

When I think of grief turned to joy, I can't help turning the pages of my Bible to John 20.

Mary Magdalene knew the healing power of the gospel firsthand. Luke 8:2 tells us that Jesus cured her of seven demons, and she was one of several women who traveled with Jesus and the disciples from town to village with the news that God's kingdom had come. Mark tells us Mary Magdalene was watching when Jesus died. Matthew tells us she was one of the women who came forward to care for his body before it was laid in the tomb. And both Luke and John feature Mary Magdalene on that Sunday morning when the stone was rolled away from the cave tomb.

Mary Magdalene knew Jesus was dead. She saw his death with her own eyes. She was there when Joseph of Arimathea and Nicodemus took charge of preparing Jesus' body for burial. This involved yards and yards of cloth and pounds and pounds of spices. John 19:39 tells us Nicodemus bought seventy-five pounds of myrrh and aloes. Perhaps Mary Magdalene's own hands rubbed the ointments into Jesus' skin.

The clock ticked on the Jewish Sabbath, which began on Friday night. To keep the Sabbath, the preparers had to interrupt their task and watch as Jesus was laid in a tomb and guards took up their stations outside so there could be no "funny business" with the body of this controversial character. Jesus was dead, no question about it.

When the Sabbath was over, on Sunday morning, Mary Magdalene and her friends bought even more spices to anoint Jesus' body. A Sabbath of mournful quiet had not dispelled their grief. They went to the grave expecting to continue to express their love for Jesus by further anointing his body with new spices. They just wanted closure. Yes, Jesus was dead.

Even when Mary Magdalene looked into the tomb and saw that it was empty, she did not consider it the result of a resurrection. Her grief was intensified by the reality—she thought—that someone had stolen Jesus' body. Mary ran to Peter and John and said, "They have taken the Lord's body out of the tomb, and we don't know where they have put him!" (John 20:2). The men made a mad dash to the tomb, with Mary Magdalene right behind them. By this time she was wailing. "Jesus is dead! Why can't his enemies leave him in peace?"

Mary Magdalene looked in the tomb. John tells us she saw two white-robed angels, who ask her, "Why are you crying?" Mary's eyes were still closed to the truth. She was so convinced that Jesus was dead and that

*Through Circle of Friends I have been able to connect with two ladies for the purpose of accountability. Meeting to share bits of our lives in specific and intentional ways has done incredible things for me. I have been continually stretched—and comforted. We have our own "Top Ten" list of questions that guide us through each week. Our time together truly enables us to focus on helping each other to just keep growing into the women God created us to be. We learn together about the questions that seem to be such an ongoing struggle. What a joy to be able to pray for one another in those specific areas. What a joy to praise God together for his work in our lives. —Libby*

someone had stolen his body that even the sight of two angels in the tomb didn't make her reconsider. She had no thought of resurrection. Jesus was dead. She just wanted to know where his body was.

Then she saw someone standing in the garden, and this man also asked her, "Why are you crying?" Maybe he saw something, she thought. Maybe he helped move the body. "Tell me where you have put him," she pleaded. Mary's grief was deeply entrenched. She couldn't see through her tears to the joy right before her eyes.

And then he said her name. Just her name. *Mary.* And in that moment, she recognized him. Grief melted away as joy rushed in.

How much fun it must have been for Jesus to reveal himself to her. The loss and grief and horror of his absence were null and void. A 180-degree turn. Transformation. A glimpse of glory.

## JESUS IS THE JOY.

The day we buried my aunt and my cousin's husband was bright and bone-chillingly cold. The day of the double funeral was also the day of the Circle of Friends conference. My aunt had purchased a ticket to the event weeks earlier, none of us imagining that by the time of the conference, Alice would know in fullness all the things she thought she might learn that day. My inclination was to stay home with my mother, who had just buried her sister, but after the funeral, she urged me to go see how the conference was going. I had already sent a note to be read explaining my absence, but Mom was curious about how things were going. So was I, and I followed her suggestion that I go find out.

The place was packed. Women were worshipping with full hearts. Other leaders of Circle of Friends encouraged me to speak to the gathering because so many people had asked how I was doing and were praying for my family, so I soon found myself on stage behind the microphone.

I thanked everyone for the outpouring of well wishes my family had received as we walked through our tragedy. I spoke of my confidence that Alice and Larry were both with Jesus and the redemption that came to my uncle even through his loss.

"Alice and Larry would be the first to say that they want you to know Jesus, too," I said. "Don't leave until you are certain."

Hands went up around the church as women acknowledged their need for Jesus. I recognized some of the people, and I knew they had family members praying for them.

How exciting to see grief turned to joy all because of Jesus!

When my aunt's birthday rolled around in April, I went to her grave. I wanted to express my love for someone I had lost. By this time, spring was in the air. Snow had melted away, leaving dirt and debris on the headstone. I knew Aunt Alice wouldn't like this to be dirty, so I looked in my trunk for paper towels and a bottle of water. I could at least clean her headstone. I remember feeling happy that I could do this for her. I don't know what people know and don't know in those moments, but we will know each other in heaven, and in my imagination I think that the Lord, in his way, can let people know that someone remembered them and they are still loved.

Perhaps that's what it was like for Mary Magdalene. She wanted to show her love for someone she lost. When she went to the tomb before dawn spread its fingers, she just wanted to do something, one last thing, for Jesus.

## OPEN YOUR EYES TO A NEW REALITY.

Do our spirits long to be united with Jesus the way Mary Magdalene longed to be with him? She was a finite imperfect human being, but the joy she felt when she saw Jesus and knew him was overwhelming. Someday, when we are released from our sinful state, we will see Jesus as he really is. What will that be like? Surely it will be ultimate grief turned to joy.

The ministry of Circle of Friends helps women move through the hard places and come out on the other end with a stronger relationship with the Lord. God accepts you as you are and invites you into an adventure of relationship with him. God's vision for your life challenges you to risk exchanging the familiar for the extraordinary. No one else is you, and God gives you gifts to enrich the lives of those around you. As you go deeper into relationship with God and others, you will discover the freedom that comes from telling the truth. In God's hands, the griefs of your life can become resurrection joy.

Fear is not the last word. That's what Mary Magdalene learned on that resurrection morning. She feared that someone had taken Jesus' body, and her fear blinded her to the signs that life could be different than what she expected. When Jesus called her name, she discovered the joy of his presence. Whatever you're afraid of, don't let it blind you to the possibility of a new reality. Jesus is calling your name, too. Hear the love in his voice and turn your heart toward him.

I've said it before, and I'll say it again. We do not invite you to find a place to belong for the sake of being comfortable. Rather, in a place to belong you can see the beauty in your own scars because of what God is doing in your life, even if the process is painful. In a place to belong, you are accountable to those who journey with you. Finding an accountability partner, or a small accountability group, is an important step. We often talk about this in our Circle of Friends ministry. These friends can help you see God's redemptive hand in the challenges that seem to overwhelm. A circle of friends is not just a place to hang out and forget your troubles. It's a context for growing through your troubles and continuing to respond to God's wooing of your heart.

## 20

# THE BLESSING OF ACCOUNTABILITY

*Accountability is not judgment.*

My friend Beth smiles a lot. Some people think it's a fake smile, as if no one could possibly be that happy. But Beth is *that* happy. Beth is one of my closest friends, and she's no fake. She's one of the people in my life who asks pointed questions and keeps me accountable to my relationships and ministry.

Beth is not one of those friends who tells me I'm doing everything right. She's not one of those friends who thinks I always make perfect choices. She's not one of those friends who just wants to boast about her own accomplishments or dump about her problems.

Beth is an accountability partner. We tell each other truth about what's going on in our lives and ask each other the tough questions about how we're responding. After ten years together, we are the definition of *transparent* in our relationship.

Early on, we had a couple of other people in our accountability group. Andrea is a faithful bulldozer—a humble bulldozer, a foot-washing bulldozer—but determined nevertheless. She once confronted me over an emotional issue and said, "You're going to renounce this right now!" Some people might think she comes on too strong, but I would trust Andrea with my life.

Our fourth partner was Becky. When we invited Becky into our group while she was going through a difficult time in her life, we gave her a six-week option to drop out, because we talked about everything. And I mean *everything*. Not everybody can handle that. The group turned out to be a good fit for Becky for several years.

We were four distinct personality types. Suppose a bull came into your house and crashed around. Andrea would take the bull by the horns, wrestle it to the ground, and serve it for dinner. Becky would say, "It's okay, Mr. Bull, would you like a drink of water?" Beth would be oblivious that a bull was in the room. And I would say, "Okay, Mr. Bull, what happened in your past that made you want to do this?"

You need a few friends to whom you can say anything and everything. You don't have to broadcast the details of your life to large groups of people. Even plastic wrap is protective. You can see through it and see what's there, but it's still protective. But even more, you can be the woman to whom others can tell everything. If people perceive you as being safe, then they'll be honest with you. The question is not only, "Who can I trust?" but also, "Can others trust me?"

## EVERYBODY HAS A STORY.

Women you know are on all sorts of life journeys. Everybody has a story, and our lives crisscross each other's paths with opportunities for deep and satisfying relationships. Not everybody is in the same life situation as you are, yet you would be surprised at the people who can enrich your life.

Cheryl is in her early forties and single by choice. Not willing to settle for an unsatisfying relationship in order to be married, she has a full life of work and travel, and she realizes that she enjoys a degree of freedom that married women don't have. Still, she has her moments of loneliness. I go home from our times together to a family, and she goes home to an empty house. Diagnosed with a rare form of cancer, Cheryl faced a double mastectomy, chemotherapy, and reconstructive surgery. Through it all, she never missed a beat. If I had to face what she's faced, I hope I would respond with the measure of grace, humor, and trust that Cheryl has. She's a godly woman with an incredible sense of humor, warmth, and intelligence. Although our journeys are not the same, we enrich each other's lives.

DeeAnn is a divorced mother of three adult children. She was married for almost thirty years to a man who continues to struggle with emotional issues. Of all the divorced women I've encountered, DeeAnn went through divorce the right way. So often the temptation is to trash the husband, and friends hop right on the bandwagon. We agree how terrible his actions were and he's a horrible person—and then we go home to our husbands and that woman goes home to isolation or single parenting. DeeAnn wanted to take every opportunity to bring healing into the relationship. She entreated a few close friends, including me, to listen to her but not trash her husband. She trusted us to go deeper with her than simply agreeing she didn't deserve what was happening, but to balance truth and emotion and to walk at her side through the process of forgiveness.

My mother was in her seventies when her sister, my aunt Alice, died in an automobile accident. The loss propelled her into a group of women, and now in her senior years, she has developed some of the closest relationships she's ever had with other women.

Everybody has a story. Relationships of accountability mean we can step into each other's stories without sniffing out the salacious factor, but instead point each other toward the fullness of life God wants for each of us.

Are you an oasis in the desert or a candle in a fireworks store? Do you offer safety and healing or nudge people one step closer to disaster? Can you hear whatever someone needs to say without jumping to judgment, without offering flippant advice, and without giving in to the urge to pass on gossip?

## ACCOUNTABILITY HELPS US AVOID PITFALLS.

People who are hurting have a tendency to become manipulative. And if they are already dealing with feelings of abandonment because of the circumstances that caused their pain, they may be especially sensitive to what they perceive as further abandonment by someone else—you, for instance. I've had to learn that we who minister relationally must be aware of our own weaknesses and our own triggers. When God gives you the opportunity to influence another person, stay that much closer to God and remember

God opposes the proud and gives grace to the humble (James 4:6). When someone invites you into her struggles, it's far too easy to assume a savior mentality and try to fix things. You're not God. And what the person needs most is God. You can be obedient to the role God gives you, which includes encouraging your friend to depend on God, without trying to take over God's job. Remember that you want to lead the person to the foot of the cross, not to a relationship that raises you up or strokes your ego.

Accountability is important once we take up the mantle of God's calling on our lives, whatever it is. Believe it or not, it's possible to become addicted to affirmation. If we get high, so to speak, on being needed, danger lurks around the next corner. We can get emotionally addicted to being in the role of leader as well. Our identity is first and foremost in Christ. It is a blessing to walk in one's calling obediently, but be careful not to get sucked into a power trip in the use of your gifts. We all need to be encouraged, but we must remember that God is the one who gives gifts and calls us into pathways to use them.

Let me also give a word of warning to married women in ministry. If you allow your ministry to make you an ineffectual wife or mother, then I don't believe God will honor your actions in the long term. He gives us grace and opportunities, but *no* is not a dirty word. I often say, "I can't, but I'd like to introduce you to someone who could." In doing this, I am introducing two people to the possibilities God has for them, without feeling that I am indispensable. Nothing thrills my heart more than to be the courier of invitation to take the first step of faith and encourage people to be part of

---

*My life has been forever changed by the acceptance shown to me by founders of Circle of Friends. Years ago, when Circle of Friends was only a vague idea of God's leading, I was part of an accountability group that accepted me for who I was during a difficult time. I was caring for my mother who was suffering from ALS, and these friends stood beside me asking tough questions and showing by words and actions the love I so needed. They graciously allowed me the same freedom in their lives. Our ministry lives have taken separate turns, but I still count them as some of my best friends. These ladies not only talked about accountability and acceptance, but also practiced it for years even before the ministry had a name. —Becky*

something bigger than themselves.

Submit your will to God, and he will give you instruction and introduce you to people who will amaze you with their abilities. Know your own weaknesses so you can be encouragement and godly affirmation to another woman who is gifted and called to do what you can't. A group of people close to you can help you discern your own gifts and calling—and whether it's the right time. But if you're not willing to be accountable to someone else, you will miss out on the richness of this process. If you're not willing to admit you have shortcomings or limits in your life, it will be hard for others to help you find God's path. Whatever the demands of your life circumstances or ministry involvement, accountability helps keep you on track. People who know you will watch out for you and help you avoid the pitfalls we all know are out there.

## ACCOUNTABILITY IS MUTUAL.

I like *The Message* wording of Romans 12:10: "Be good friends who love deeply; practice playing second fiddle." Enjoy what I call your "Ethel Mertz days." On the classic 1950s sitcom "I Love Lucy," Lucy Ricardo had a best friend, Ethel Mertz. Lucy was full of big ideas and wild schemes, and Ethel was often the one who helped make them happen. Some personalities shine brighter in the spotlight and draw people to a big idea. But the Ethel Mertzes are just as important. Ethel is an example of unconditional love, loyalty, and friendship without having to always be the big idea. In fact, Ethel sometimes was the voice of caution and accountability to Lucy's wild rides. Even when Lucy got everyone in a mess—on a weekly basis—Ethel was there at her side loving her just the same.

The word *accountability* gets a bad reputation. It smacks of judgment, as if the person to whom we are accountable gets to tell us if we are bad or good. For many people, the word carries overtones of someone else being in charge and demanding accountability by calling the shots. You're accountable to a boss who gets to decide if you are doing a good job. You're accountable to a teacher who gets to decide if your effort is worthy of recognition. Accountability often seems one-sided or authoritarian.

But I'm talking about a mutual kind of accountability. Rather than trying to perform to meet someone's external standard, accountability builds on relationships rooted in trust and choice. You can *choose* to be honest with other people and invite their feedback. You can *choose* to have transparent relationships with a few close friends. Friends call each other back from the edges of pride, confusion, and discouragement. Friends launch each other into unknown territory and walk hand in hand where there is no map.

Accountability can be scary. You may feel like a small child jumping off the side of the pool with your eyes squeezed shut, not really sure if your daddy is going to catch you. But if you can't trust anybody in your life, how can you find out what could happen when you take the leap into meaningful relationships and ministry?

Accountability is not judgment. It's companionship on the journey, and it sets you free.

## 21

# No Extra Credit for
# Holding Up Alone

*I care for you. You care for me.*

My spiritual dad, Dan, called me and said, "You need to come for lunch." He was right. The last year or so of my life had drained me. My mother-in-law died, then my father-in-law, then my aunt and my cousin's husband in that horrible accident. I spent a lot of time with my cousin Kim and in comforting my mother as well. My sister had gone through a difficult divorce, and I wanted to comfort and encourage her also. Sometimes we don't process our own grief because we want to be available to someone else who is grieving. That's what I was doing, and Dan could see the damage in my own life.

Around that time, Circle of Friends received an opportunity to develop a morning radio show in Canton, Ohio. Several of us rotated leadership and developed a group format in the summer of 2007. It was an exciting time but emotionally demanding. I was also hosting a daily program for the Moody network at the same time.

Personal loss, one after another.

Ministry demands.

Daily life with a family and a business.

I was stretched thin, and Dan knew it. His invitation to come for lunch was a gentle nudge toward being accountable to take care of myself. I wanted to go, but one thing after another interfered, and the summer weeks blew by. It was the middle of August by the time I finally made the drive to the town where Dan lived, and we settled in at an Old English tearoom that he and his wife enjoyed. The food was wonderful, the atmosphere relaxing.

Dan had a ministry of encouragement and intercession through prayer, and he took advantage of the unusual demands of his own schedule to use these gifts. He was only sixty-six that summer, but already he had been through two open-heart surgeries and was on dialysis because of damage to his kidneys. He went to dialysis at four in the morning several times a week and used those hours to be with the Lord and pray for the people God put on his heart. As much as he didn't like the physical process of dialysis, he relished those quiet hours with God. I had been on his heart all summer.

In the tearoom, Dan opened his Bible, which he always had with him, because he knew the Word of God could have more impact than anything he might say. He turned the pages to Isaiah 30 and read to me.

> *The LORD must wait for you to come to him so he can show you his love and compassion. For the LORD is a faithful God. Blessed are those who wait for his help. O people of Zion, who live in Jerusalem, you will weep no more. He will be gracious if you ask for help. He will surely respond to the sound of your cries. Through the LORD gave you adversity for food and suffering for drink, he will still be with you to teach you. You will see your teacher with your own eyes.* (Isaiah 30:18–20)

Dan also read to me from Psalm 46:10: "Be still, and know that I am God! I will be honored by every nation. I will be honored throughout the world."

Dan's admonition for me that day was not to substitute the work of ministry for intimacy with God. "When the Lord is using you in powerful ways to speak love and acceptance," he said, "it's easy to make the work of ministry an idol. Anything that comes between you and time with the Lord—watch out. God is a jealous God!"

He had another verse from the Psalms for me: "You keep track of all my sorrows. You have collected all my tears in your bottle. You have recorded each one in your book" (Psalm 56:8).

"That verse keeps coming to my heart concerning you," Dan said. "You've been through a sorrowful season. That receptacle is there waiting to hold the tears you haven't shed yet."

Dan knew me well. Self-care is crucial for people who deal with depression, and those close to me recognize that I'm not very good about it. Dan could see that I had gotten to the point of stuffing my grief rather than living through it. I was so numb I couldn't even cry, though I'd had reason after reason to cry. Dan could see how hollow I'd become over the last year.

"I think you'll find a place of peace if you get alone with the Lord and let him minister to you," Dan continued. "Get some of that cleaned out. You keep pressing on because there are things that need to be done. The grace of God gives you strength for the day. Now it's time to be with God and let him have your tears." Dan felt a burden from God to pray for me and ask God to sustain me until the time came when I was ready to deal with the realities building up inside me. He loved me enough to remind me that God loves me and I don't have to be a super-personality who can take hit after hit without flinching. In fact, Dan was reminding me of my responsibility to take care of myself.

Dan was convalescing from a medical procedure, so I was driving that day. He sat in the same seat where my aunt Alice had sat a few months earlier pouring out her heartache about Uncle Don's salvation. As I dropped him at his office, he told me that he faced another medical procedure.

"I'm just asking the Lord about this valve replacement. Maybe I'm not going to be here very long." Dan knew that dialysis is hard on the body and shortens life span.

I took his face in my hands. "Thank you. You know how much I love you."

A week later, Dan phoned to let me know he was going to undergo a cardiac catheterization, an outpatient procedure. On the day of the procedure, everything went fine. When he and his wife got home in the afternoon, she stepped into the other room while Dan stayed in the kitchen to flip through the mail.

She heard him gasp.

And that fast, he was gone because of a blood clot.

I sang at his graveside service a few days later with my guitar. But I did not cry.

## TEARS DO CLEANSING WORK.

Years earlier I had met a wonderful woman named Faith Jones. She was a therapist who helped me face up to the long-lasting impact of the sexual harassment I suffered during high school and work my way through the eating disorder and depression issues. This was before Circle of Friends became an organized ministry, but early on, Faith caught the vision for what might be. Once I was no longer in a therapeutic relationship with Faith, we began a friendship to the extent that we could without violating the state ethical standards of her profession. The years passed, and we were finally outside the window of time when anyone could object to our working together. By this time, Circle of Friends was up and running, and we knew we wanted to add a counseling component to our ministry. Faith was ready to make a change, too. We provided office space for Faith to see clients under the Circle of Friends umbrella.

> I was concerned about a situation, and I called my friend. She patiently listened to my struggle, talked it out, and prayed with me. She is a great accountability partner. She cares, she is genuine, and I know she loves me, because she walks with me as God refines my soul. I can tell her things and know it will go no further. It makes me smile to look at her picture when I hear her on the radio program. —Kay

Faith was there in the capacity of a ministry partner and friend when Aunt Alice and Larry died. She was continually asking me how I was doing. I would answer flatly, "I feel bad, but I'm okay." But Faith knew I was not okay. During that busy summer of 2007 in the wake of the tragedy, often when Faith had a break between clients, she would ask if I wanted to chat. She went out of her way to make herself available to me. When Dan died, I just kept going, putting one foot in front of the other. But Faith knew this was a huge moment for me.

Finally, Faith called me into her office and got directly to the point. "You need to take some time off. You've had some incredible losses in the last year and a half, but you just keep going. That's admirable, but you're going to burn out, and I'm concerned."

"Why now?" I asked. "What am I doing that concerns you?"

"Have you cried lately?"

I shrugged. "I feel sad, but I don't feel like crying." My friend Beth had asked me about crying as well, and I gave her the same answer.

Faith wasn't going to let it go. "That's more of a concern to me than if you were crying and couldn't stop. If you're in such deep grief that you can't even cry, you really need to take some time. What do you do when you're alone?"

The truth was that when I was alone, I was content to sit in my living room all day with the lights off and stare out the window.

"I'm going to write a letter to your ministry employers," Faith said, "recommending a hiatus for your own emotional and physical health."

"Uh, okay."

I expected simply to be fired. I had already stopped being on-air in the Canton program, leaving it in the capable hands of other women from Circle of Friends. Telling the people at Moody that I needed at least six weeks off would create a burden for them. I would understand if they preferred to find a permanent replacement. Happily for me, they chose to wait for me.

I still didn't cry. I just started to stay home. I'd get the kids off to school and just be alone in the house. The words of Isaiah 30:18 floated through my brain. The Lord was waiting for me to come to him so he could be gracious. *How do you want to be gracious to me?* I asked. But I did not sense an answer. I did the usual household tasks and took lots of drives in the sunny autumn days of changing leaves. It took me about two weeks of just being in a quiet place in my spirit before the numbness started to wear off.

I still did not cry.

One day I started looking through baby pictures. My son, Christian, was an easy baby and very typical in the early months. But as I looked at his pictures, I could see when he began to transition into looking like a child on the spectrum of autism disorders.

That's what made me cry. Grief and mourning flowed out of me at last. But it was not grief like someone who has no hope. I kept looking at pictures and remembering specific days, and I could see what God was doing in Christian's life even in difficult situations. My hope was in the Lord. My longing for heaven increased. I love my life, but when it's time to go home, I won't mind.

I'd also go to the cemetery during those weeks for moments of re-membrance and thanksgiving—and yes, grief—for those I had lost. My friend Andrea, part of my original accountability group, had moved to another state, and I went to visit her. Beth and I spent time together. My parents, sisters, and husband all knew God was using this time to draw me to him and heal my heart. They patiently waited for the cleansing work of tears.

After a few weeks, part of me longed to go back to a normal schedule and part of me was afraid to do so. Gradually I stepped back into my life.

## "Are you okay?" Answer the question.

I don't know about you, but sometimes I would prefer to work my way around situations rather than plow through the fallow ground of the heart. That's what I was doing when I couldn't cry. Somehow we think that if we just keep going, things won't hurt as much. We see what we can do for someone else, and we do that. We see new ministry opportunities, and we respond. We give our time and energy to our families. We go to work. And in the process we build a wall around our hearts and hang a sign that says, "I'm okay."

Except we're not.

There's no extra credit in the righteousness column for trying to go it alone. I am blessed to have people in my life who were not afraid to speak the truth to me. They could see what I did not want to acknowledge for myself, and they didn't quit on me. They kept asking, "Are you okay?" and after about the hundredth time, I finally admitted I wasn't.

A few weeks of a reduced schedule, rich conversation with people who knew me well, time to be still in God's presence—I needed all these things more than I realized. In my case I also benefited from an evaluation of the medications that treat my depression.

I can hear some of you saying, "Yeah, six weeks off sounds great. But it's not going to happen for me. You don't know my life."

Don't miss the point here. I'm not telling you this story of a painful time in my life because I think you should take two months off from your life. I want you to recognize the signs that you are headed for the pit I was in and take care of yourself so you don't have to go there! I'm sharing my experience so that you can look at your life and perhaps consider the warning signs that you are becoming numb.

Numb to joy.

Numb to adventure.

Numb to yourself.

Numb to God.

I lost five people close to me within a year and a half. That's a lot of grief to leave unprocessed. But other experiences cause grief as well. You may be experiencing extreme relational stress or gulping for financial air. You may be caught in a work situation that sucks the life out of you. Maybe you have a child who makes you pull your hair out or aging parents who seem to need more from you every week. Perhaps you have a child with special needs and you grieve the future.

Some of us have a tendency to look at our lives, compare them with someone else's circumstances, and conclude, "Well, I don't have it as bad as she does. At least I don't have cancer for the third time." "At least my husband didn't leave me." "At least my child didn't die." And so we keep plodding on.

This is not a contest, my friends. Suffering is suffering. The psalmist tells us God keeps track of all our sorrows. He records *each one*. He doesn't cast some of them aside as not worthy of his sympathy or classify some as not worth spilling tears over. You don't have to just buck up and bear it. God cares that you're suffering.

Taking care of myself is something I struggle with in general, so I'm grateful for friends who speak up and remind me. This is the loving arm of accountability. This is the companionship of accountability. This is the humility of accountability. If your journey is leading you through a tunnel right now, you don't have to go there alone. When someone asks how you are, answer the question and see what happens! And if you know someone who is in a tunnel, care enough to take her hand and walk with her.

## 22

# AT THE FEET OF JESUS

*Jesus shows the way to truth.*

Have you ever thought that Martha got a bad rap? After all, if you have a house full of guests, somebody has to put a meal on the table. And is it really fair that all the work should fall to Martha when Mary is capable of at least getting the dishes ready?

This is the scene we enter in Luke 10:38–42. Jesus was on a journey to Jerusalem and stopped in the village of Bethany to see his friends. Two sisters, Mary and Martha, and their brother, Lazarus, lived in Bethany. This was the same Lazarus whom Jesus would later raise from the dead. Apparently Jesus had a genuine friendship with this group of siblings, since the gospel writers record several stories of his visits to Bethany.

Luke tells us Martha "welcomed him into her home." But remember, Jesus did not travel alone. He had as many as twelve male disciples with him as he roamed the countryside, and a number of women followed his movements as well. So when Martha welcomed Jesus, she welcomed his entourage. This was not the sort of thing where you could just get out last night's leftover pot roast and paper plates.

I think we should admire Martha's warm hospitality. She opened her home and her heart to Jesus and set out being efficient with the practicalities of her own ministry to him. Clearly she was interested in honoring her guest and his friends. In fact, in the culture of the time, it would have been shameful not to feed them. She wanted to do the right thing in serving Jesus.

Mary also wanted to welcome Jesus, and she went about it in a completely different way. She stayed *out* of the kitchen. Cooking just didn't seem important. She was not counting silverware or pressing the tablecloth or laying dishes. Instead, she sat at Jesus' feet the way a student would sit at the feet of a teacher so as not to miss a word.

Some of us might prefer to sit next to Jesus, alongside him. Mary chose a submissive position that acknowledged there was a lot she didn't know that Jesus could teach her. Sitting at his feet also strikes me as intimate. Mary felt comfortable with Jesus. It was safe to put herself at his feet and be completely engrossed in his presence.

This is where Martha's intentions drifted off course. She started out trying to do the right thing. Perhaps she assumed others—her sister in particular—would share her priorities of serving Jesus through a good hearty meal. It seemed obvious to Martha that this is what needed to be done. So when Mary didn't read Martha's mind and chose instead to sit at Jesus' feet, Martha fumed. She checked the progress of her culinary creations, got the best platters down from the high shelf, wiped the spots off the wine goblets, all the while shooting darts at her sister with her eyes. But Mary wasn't getting the hint, and finally Martha couldn't take it anymore. Now she didn't even want to talk to her sister. In her mind, the offense had grown so grievous, it was a matter for Jesus.

"Lord," she said to Jesus, "doesn't it seem unfair to you that my sister just sits here while I do all the work? Tell her to come and help me" (Luke 10:40).

Now Martha crossed the line. All her good intentions to serve and honor Jesus got lost in her resentment at the workload. There's nothing wrong with being a motivated, proactive worker, especially when we do it out of a desire to please God. But if we choose to minister in that fashion, we have to be careful not to get frustrated with others who do not share our temperament. Martha's mistake was not in working hard to put a good meal on the table, but in letting someone else's calling get in the way of serving with joy herself. Martha's busyness overstretched her, and she lost sight of what she was really trying to do in the first place. Honoring Jesus had morphed into an unfair pile of work.

Look at the contrast between how these two sisters related to Jesus. Martha had a plan—a good, worthy plan—but when others didn't execute it to her satisfaction, she *told* Jesus what he *should* say to someone else. Mary, on the other hand, sat at Jesus' feet and *listened* to what Jesus *chose* to say. Martha thought her sister was "just sitting there." She completely missed the point of what Mary was doing.

Mary didn't criticize Martha for fussing in the kitchen, but she recognized her own need simply to be in Jesus' presence and learn from him. It wasn't so much that Mary didn't want to serve Jesus, but that she didn't want anything to get in the way of being with him.

We can understand this from a human perspective. Even in the context of my own marriage, I can tell everyone how wonderful Bob is and what a difference he's made in my life. But I also want to spend time with him. One of the best days we ever spent together was in southern Texas. We were there for a business convention and took a day for ourselves. On a rented motorcycle, we rode around wherever we felt like going. We had such a good time just being in one another's presence. When we think of banner days in our life, that's one of them. The activity was nothing extraordinary. The joy came from just being together. We were being intentional about being with each other because we love each other.

Spending that day with my husband taught me a lot about what I miss out on when I don't just chill with Bob. I can be so driven, and all for a good cause. Bob appreciates my ministry, and he appreciates hearing the favorable things I have to say about him. But at the end of the day, he says, "Better still, I like that when you come home you actually pay attention to me."

Nobody loves us more than Jesus, so why do we so easily neglect just being with Jesus?

In Luke 10, Jesus did not actually address the issue of who was supposed to feed him. The reality is somebody had to do the work of preparing the meal. But in his answer to Martha, Jesus made it clear that he was not going to ask Mary to give up spending time with him in order to go make herself useful in the other room. He said, "My dear Martha, you are worried and upset over all these details! There is only one thing worth being concerned about. Mary has discovered it—and it won't be taken away from her" (Luke 10:41–42).

## Find the best of Martha and Mary.

Martha's story highlights the tension so many of us feel between being preoccupied with practicalities—including our ministries—and abiding with God with no agenda. How often do we try to tell God what to do to make our ministries better? Are we so different from Martha?

We do have to do the practical things. That's a fact of life. We all need to eat, and many of us are responsible for the care and feeding of others who depend on us. Phone calls, e-mails, practice sessions, reading material—the practical work has to be done. I don't think Jesus was ignoring that reality. I think he expected a meal when he showed up at Martha's house. The point Jesus makes in this story, however, is not to let the activities of our lives and ministry get us so flustered that we lose track of why we're doing them in the first place. Sometimes we need to just let go of things and sit with Mary at the feet of Jesus. We need to hear the Word of God. We need to learn from what Jesus has to say to us. We need fresh reminders that we are part of the kingdom of God in the here and now, and our lives should reflect the priorities of the kingdom of God.

> *I found a place to grow and be stretched when I found a circle of friends who would speak truth in love and hold me accountable in areas that are most important to me: my relationship with God and his people. —Beth*

Jocelyn is one of my friends and co-laborers in Circle of Friends. I hear her say over and over, "The Lord is so precious." When she says this, I hear the voice of a woman who has spent time with Jesus. She speaks of him as the closest of friends. She basks in his presence. Jocelyn has an incredible husband who loves the Lord, but Jesus is the lover of her soul.

Jocelyn came from a family of divorce. The youngest of five children, she was just twelve when her parents split up. She felt her father's absence, and her mother was emotionally unable to supply the support and affirmation and nurturing that a twelve-year-old daughter needed. Jocelyn is quick to admit she went through a season of confusion and rebellion. But when she finally understood the measure of love Jesus has for her and the dependability of his character, her heart was captured. She's an incredible Bible teacher who draws women to the feet of Jesus. She carries the essence of Jesus in her person, and it shows on her face. People are drawn to her because she sparkles with Holy Spirit glitter, and she leads them right to Jesus.

I love God more deeply because he has allowed me to know Jocelyn. She doesn't just say she wants to spend time with the Lord; she actually does it. And she protects that time. Busyness does not infringe on time she intentionally sets aside to be with God. Jocelyn spends a lot of time preparing Bible studies to share with others, but I'm always curious to see where her own Bible is open to and what she is underlining. Hers is a Bible where you see an ongoing conversation. She's a living example of a Mary at the feet of Jesus.

## GET A WHIFF OF JESUS.

Martha's relationship with Jesus continued to grow after Jesus redirected her attention where it belongs. In John 11, we read the startling story of Jesus raising Lazarus from the dead. Martha says to Jesus, "I have always believed you are the Messiah, the Son of God, and the one who has come into the world from God" (John 11:27). And then, in the next chapter, Martha is once again serving a dinner for Jesus in her home (John 12:2). This time we don't hear any objection from Martha about the choice her sister makes. Mary takes a jar of expensive perfume and pours it over Jesus' feet. Then she wipes his feet with her hair.

That bottle of perfume was worth a year's wages, so it was no small gift given with a grudging heart. This was a beautiful act of worship and humility. Mary could have poured the perfume over Jesus' head, which was the more common gesture, but she chose to pour it over his feet. Cleaning the feet of a dinner guest normally was a servant's task, but Mary wanted to do it herself out of her love for Jesus. Martha had not stopped serving, but she seemed to have learned that Mary understood the heart of honoring Jesus.

John tells us the house was filled with the fragrance of Mary's perfume. I love perfume—probably too much. I don't feel dressed if I don't have perfume on. The fragrance of Christ is something I want to put on, and I want it to last until after I'm gone from that place. I have a friend whose son claims he can smell my presence an hour after I've gone. When I step into my husband's embrace, I smell his aftershave fragrance. When I get close, I get a good whiff of someone who loves me. I want it to be that way with Jesus. I want to get close enough to get a good whiff of him, and I want the scent to linger in the air. Then when people come close to me, I want them to get a good whiff of Jesus who loves them.

Closeness means different things to different people. God can translate closeness into a relationship however he wants to. For me it's just sitting quietly and knowing that every beat of my heart is a gift from God. I sit still in his presence, at his feet, and think on who he is. Infinite. All-knowing. Unconditionally loving. Creator of the universe. Why wouldn't I want to spend more time asking him how to live my life and to make me aware of opportunities, instead of falling into Martha's trap of just doing the next thing to get everything right?

## WALK THROUGH THE GOSPELS WITH JESUS.

The most productive part of a relationship with God is just being with God. I love to tell people to walk through the Gospels with Jesus. Read the Gospels—Matthew, Mark, Luke, and John—from the perspective of tagging along everywhere that Jesus goes. Listen to what he says. Watch what he does. See his relationships with people. Notice when he's tired and how he handles pressure and what happens when he draws away to be alone with his Father. Experience life with Jesus.

One of the greatest gifts accountability partners can give one another is to keep pointing back to the feet of Jesus. Whether your distractions come from caring for small children, running the soccer league, operating a business, or keeping a ministry fresh and vibrant, busyness can overwhelm. "Spend time with Jesus" is on the list but never quite makes it to the top. I don't say this to put a guilt trip on you, but to challenge you to recognize the very well-intentioned activities in your life that nevertheless pull you off track. Telling someone else how this happens might be the first step toward making mid-course corrections. Accountability is not about shaming each other into better behavior, but encouraging one another as we walk the path together.

Perhaps you recognize yourself in Martha. Maybe you could really use someone to consistently check in to see how you're spending time learning from Jesus. Knowing that someone is going to ask might get you over the hump and help bring balance to your life.

A friend's face may be floating through your mind right now, someone who works hard to serve God and others but is losing herself in the process. How can you lovingly reach out and encourage her?

Listen to your own voice when you talk to others about your life and ministry. Are you complaining about how much work it is—which is culturally acceptable behavior these days—or do others see how wholly devoted you are to Jesus the person?

Are you finding fresh nourishment in the Word of God, or are you spiritually living off of things you learned a long time ago? Is your life a conversation with God or more like a book report about something you read years ago?

Accountability brings the comfort of companionship. Fear and resentment about what happens in your life are not the last word. You can have a new life in Christ. Telling the truth to someone else and hearing another person's truth can set you free if you dare to do it. Accountability is an experience of love, not judgment, and it will keep you growing spiritually through the busyness and challenges of your life. Jesus shows the way to truth. Walk toward the truth with someone else at your side.

# 23

# LEARN FROM MISTAKES

*You can't stay stuck and be free.*

I once helped a friend with her son's graduation party. My assignment: the chocolate fountain! It doesn't get much better than that. A stainless steel statue flowed with luscious, rich, smooth chocolate rippling effortlessly down the sides. Quite the neat invention, if you ask me.

As I melted twenty-eight pounds of chocolate, I had ample time to stir, think, pray, stir, think some more—well, you get the picture. I was reminded that moderation isn't a bad thing. As I looked at what seemed to be a river of the "fruit" of our friend the cocoa bean, I thought, "No more for me today, thank you." Indulging in a good thing at the wrong time can make you feel pretty lousy.

At the end of the day, I had only one spot on my white shirt. What was I thinking—a white shirt and a chocolate fountain? Spray 'n Wash to the rescue! If only it were that simple to remove the blemishes spotting our lives.

## HIDING SIN ONLY MAKES IT WORSE.
The Old Testament King David knew what it was like to mess up royally. He did it more than once. On one occasion, he drew a woman named Bathsheba into his self-indulgent scheme.

On a spring afternoon, David got up from a nap and wandered out to the flat roof of his palace. He was probably looking for some cool air, or perhaps he meant to think for a few minutes about his general Joab and the troops he had sent off to battle. From the top of the palace, David could see a lot of what was going on in the neighborhood. Nearby, Bathsheba was having a bath, and as David watched, he unfortunately allowed his visual radar to lock in on her physical beauty. He sent someone to fetch her, and when she arrived, he had his way with her.

Women in that culture did not have much power, not even over their own bodies. Plus this was the king! It's easy to imagine Bathsheba did not feel she had any choice but to sleep with David. Was she flattered? Was she angered? Did she submit against her will? How did she feel the next morning? We don't know much of what she felt, since the story comes to us from David's point of view. A few weeks later, Bathsheba discovered she was pregnant. Since her husband, Uriah, is off at war with General Joab, there was no question that David fathered her child. Bathsheba did not initiate the encounter with David and likely felt she had no real option to refuse him. Nevertheless, she was left with the consequences. She was going to have his baby.

David's hormonal lack of judgment was about to become public. His efforts to fix the situation create a multifaceted disaster. David specifically asked that Uriah come home from the battlefield to give a report on how things were going. The king went through the motions of hearing the report, but what he was most anxious about was for Uriah to go home to sleep with his wife.

Imagine David's shock when he discovered that Uriah had more honor than that. The ark of the Lord, a chest representing the very presence of God among his people, was in the middle of a battle. How can Uriah think about sex at a time like that? If David had been as devout, he would not have been in the tangled web he was in at the moment. Now David went on a power trip and gave a rash command that would take care of this problem once and for all. He sent Uriah back to Joab with a brazen note that said, "Station Uriah on the front lines where the battle is fiercest. Then pull back so that he will be killed" (2 Samuel 11:15).

Faithful, honorable Uriah had no idea he was the courier of his own death sentence to Joab. He was a good man who served loyally, and this was how the king rewarded him. The next news of the battle to reach David assured him that Uriah was dead—along with other completely innocent soldiers. Who needs *The Young and the Restless* when you can read the Bible?

David had everything a man could want. Power. Influence. Good looks—the Bible says he was easy on the eyes. With all of that, why did he have to steal another man's wife, murder the man, cause the death of other innocent soldiers, and involve Joab in carrying out the carnage? David lusting after Bathsheba was akin to a diabetic staring at the chocolate fountain. Keep on looking, and more than likely there's going to be a big problem.

Bathsheba went into mourning for her husband. Her husband was in the military, so she knew he was at risk. Did she know that David had hastened Uriah's death? Or did she suspect it when she heard the news? We don't know. And she still had the king's baby growing inside her. If Bathsheba had other children with Uriah—we don't know—she still had to be the mom and keep going. She was not in a position to call the shots, but just had to wait to see what David would do.

Tragic circumstances befall people through no fault of their own. Bathsheba didn't seek an affair with David. She didn't scheme to get pregnant. She did not send her own husband to battle to be killed. None of this was her fault, but her life was coming apart at the seams. Her story might make us ask, "Where is God in situations like this?"

God is a God of justice. And life is not fair. Both statements are true. David's actions brought consequences, and he suffered. But Bathsheba also suffered those consequences even though the events were not her fault. However, God can take a sinful, tragic circumstance and bring a positive outcome.

Life is full of things we cannot undo. We can be sorry, we can have regrets, we can be the victim of someone else's choices, but we can't undo any of it. We can't change what happened. Somehow we have to move on. That is what David and Bathsheba did.

David sent for Bathsheba again, this time to make her one of his wives so she could give birth to their son as a woman married to the child's father.

We might think David breathed a sigh of relief at this point. Uriah and the other soldiers were unfortunate collateral damage, but at least he quashed the potential scandal. If anyone was counting the months, they kept their mouths shut. Everyone was just glad when the baby was born and life could move forward.

Except God did not forget. Enter Nathan, the prophet of God.

Nathan told David a story about a rich man and a poor man. The rich man had flocks and flocks of sheep, and the poor man had one little lamb. Yet when the rich man wanted to prepare a feast, he slaughtered the poor man's one little lamb.

David is furious. "Any man who would do such a thing deserves to die! He must repay four lambs to the poor man for the one he stole and for having no pity" (2 Samuel 12:5–6).

"You are that man!" Nathan pointed out.

David repented on the spot. He was finished trying to justify his actions, finally. The Lord spared David, but he caused Bathsheba's baby to fall ill, which tore David up. He fasted and prayed all night for God to spare the baby, but the child died.

Then we read that David comforted Bathsheba (2 Samuel 12:24). Again, we know little of what Bathsheba felt, but it's not difficult to imagine her devastation. After everything she had been through, now to lose the baby this way seemed unbearable. It was one more thing that she had no control over, one more consequence she had to bear because of someone else's sin. But it would seem she had found some way to forgive David if she received his comfort. It's difficult to be comforted by someone you haven't forgiven. She seems to have made peace with David and with God about what happened and moved forward with her new marriage.

Bathsheba conceived again and gave birth to Solomon, who succeeded David as king and was in the line of descendants that eventually led to the birth of Jesus. That puts Bathsheba among Jesus' ancestors, too. Solomon was a great king for much of his reign—wise and faithful to the Lord. His reputation spanned the globe. How honored do you think Bathsheba was to be the mother of Solomon? God vindicated her by allowing her to be the mother of a man who was highly esteemed by everyone who knew of him, and by making her an ancestor of Jesus.

Bathsheba's story leaves us with so many unanswered questions, but it is a good catalyst for considering how to approach moving on after suffering the consequences of someone else's choices. Do we respond to the hurt, or do we respond to the character of God? Can we take that hurt and help someone see life in a way that will bring better choices in the future?

## It's possible to move beyond the hurt.

Angela's husband had an affair. Bryan has an element of David in him—smart, knows the Word of God, professional, in church leadership. Yet he succumbed. Angela and Bryan socialized with the other woman and her husband. The wives were friends. But Bryan made a mistake, and he could quickly see how destructive his choice could be, so he confessed the relationship.

Angela was hurt and angry, of course. Devastated, actually. But she managed to step back from the situation and recognize that her children needed their father. He was a good dad, engaged in their lives. Angela was caught in the consequences of someone else's choice, and she became very depressed. Sometimes while she was driving, the temptation to let the car drift over the center line into the path of another vehicle was intense, almost irresistible. She didn't see how she could ever get back the trusting, innocent life she'd had before learning of Bryan's affair. Initially she was not sure

*My circle of friends began some sixteen years ago when I invited my friend Beth to a meeting of Mothers of Preschoolers (MOPS). What began as an invitation from one young mom to another eventually became a friendship that has truly stood the test of time. Our pastor challenged us to form an accountability group with two to four people. Beth and I believed it was the Lord's will for us to be accountable to one another and ask each other a specific set of questions about our relationship with Christ, our families, and our decision-making processes. Lisa and Becky joined our group, and together we explored the blessings that come by asking questions and speaking truth into each other's lives. —Andrea*

she could remain married to Bryan. He had hurt her too deeply. Then she opened a newspaper and saw an advertisement for a divorce lawyer. Looking at the ad made her feel like she would throw up. She knew God did not want her to divorce Bryan. She had to choose to forgive him and make changes in her own attitude about her marriage.

Angela and Bryan stayed together. They were intentional about their accountability to one another and each other's whereabouts. Do I believe she loves and trusts him? Absolutely. Does he respect her? Absolutely. The relationship they have now is a miracle. Angela has not held on to the hurt. She could not display the love and respect she has for her husband if she had not forgiven him, and her forgiveness gave him a whole new perspective on the grace and mercy of God.

Maybe that's the kind of relationship David and Bathsheba ended up having. Bathsheba suffered because of David's choices, but she seemed to forgive him and allow him to comfort her and have a family together.

As I have the honor of walking through the minefields of people's personal experiences as a lay counselor, I am constantly directed back to Psalm 25. This passage of scripture ministered to me when Dan, my spiritual dad, interceded for me with its words, and I learned to embrace the psalm as a cry out to the Lord on my own behalf. I have been able to use it to help others cry out to the Lord and ask him to show them his way and to assure them that if they trust him, they will not be ashamed or disappointed.

*O LORD, I give my life to you. I trust in you, my God! . . . Do not remember the rebellious sins of my youth. Remember me in the light of your unfailing love, for you are merciful, O LORD. . . . My eyes are always on the LORD, for he rescues me from the traps of my enemies. . . . May integrity and honesty protect me, for I put my hope in you.*
(Psalm 25:1–2, 7, 15, 21)

We do have our own part in this process of putting shame behind us and getting on God's path. We begin by asking forgiveness. David had courage to ask God for forgiveness. He knew that if God forgave him, he was truly forgiven. When God forgives, he separates us from our sin as far as the east is from the west (Psalm 103:12). To know that God can choose to forget what I've done to hurt him gives me hope that I'll be able to forgive myself.

Sometimes we have to forgive ourselves over and over again as we see the consequences our choices have led to. It's still possible to move forward and allow God to teach us in a hard situation. Even our mistakes can be God's tool to redeem another situation.

Christ absorbed my shame and guilt on the cross. This is unfathomable in my finite mind, but I know it's true. If God can forgive me, then who am I to be so prideful that I cannot forgive myself? If you are holding on to self-hatred because of something you have done in the past, it amounts to pride. You're putting yourself above God. If God declares you righteous, then how much more righteous can you be? You cannot somehow achieve a greater forgiveness of yourself than what God already offers you.

## DON'T BE STUCK. BE FREE.

What's before your eyes? What have you developed a taste for? What do you find yourself thinking about? Take a moment to ask God if it's pleasing to him. If you don't ask him now, you'll be explaining it later. Perhaps those confessions will come through tears of regret and remorse. Are you involved in something that God meant for good and you've perverted it as you act out in the energy of human flesh?

We get stuck. We get stuck in habits and indulgences that have the potential to take our lives apart piece by piece. We get stuck in the consequences of our own choices, and we get stuck in the consequences of choices we had no control over. We get stuck in unforgiveness toward people who have hurt us, and we get stuck in unforgiveness toward ourselves because of how badly we mess things up sometimes.

But you can't stay stuck and be free at the same time. Christ died to free you.

David thought he was above God's law. He knew what he was doing was wrong, and he did it anyway, and a lot of people got hurt. The story of his relationship with Bathsheba has so much potential for getting stuck and not seeing God's redeeming hand. But David had Nathan in his life. The prophet was the king's accountability partner. Nathan told David the truth. Nathan called him to confront what he had done rather than pretend it never happened. Nathan pointed David toward God's forgiveness. Nathan pointed David toward God's redemption. Instead of getting stuck, David and Bathsheba were set free.

So many people are afraid of the word *accountability,* and if they react to a harmless word, imagine how they feel about the process of being accountable to someone. But rather than fencing us in, accountability helps set us free to discover God at work in our lives.

Come as you really are to God. Risk being real with someone else. Explore what God wants you to do with your life. And remember that the comfort of companionship in your journey—yes, through accountability—can be one of the most freeing experiences of your life.

# WHERE YOUR LOVE BEGINS

Lord, I know Your ways are not my own.
There is nothing good within me.
Feel so far, as the east is from the west,
Surely too far from Your mercy.

Locked inside,
Pain and loneliness that words can't speak,
Your pure love sets me free.

Even in the darkest moments,
When it seems that all my hope is gone,
Even in the depths of sadness,
And I know my heart just can't go on,
You call my name.
When I've reached the end,
You call my name.
That's where your love begins.

Lord, you know such shame and emptiness,
For you were beaten and rejected.
Still you carried my shame onto the cross,
There forever you left it.

Peace within,
Washed in springs of everlasting love,
Can such love ever be?

# Reflections

❧ How do the words of this song connect with your life?

❧ Honestly evaluate your personal motivation for telling people about the hard places in your life. Is it to get sympathy, or do you welcome challenging questions?

❧ It's hard to admit our own shortcomings. In what areas of your life and relationships do you need someone to help you through honest conversation?

❧ How do the concepts of "mutuality" and "choice" affect your understanding of what it means to be accountable to another person?

❧ How well do you take care of yourself in the midst of your other responsibilities? When someone asks, "Are you okay?" do you tell the truth? Why or why not?

❧ Where might you be stuck in your spiritual growth? How might a relationship of accountability help set you free?

# ACTION

We pray you will step into your journey.
Walk in your purpose.

# 24

# Rahab the Risk Taker

*This is your moment.*

Your journey into a circle of friends begins when you embark on an adventure in relationship. You come as you are to God and receive his *acceptance*, and you realize other people are ready to walk alongside you in discovering what God wants to do with your life. With the security of this acceptance, you begin to exchange the familiar for the extraordinary by experiencing *authenticity* with the people walking with you. You tell each other the truth. This leads to *affirmation*, and you enrich the lives around you because you know that no one else is you and God gives you gifts to do what he calls you to do. Because all of us realize that the demands of our lives can make the path fuzzy at times, relationships of *accountability* help us find truth at the feet of Jesus over and over.

These are key principles of the ministry of Circle of Friends, and these principles can make a difference in your life. Acceptance, authenticity, affirmation, and accountability make us bold to step out in *action*. As individual women find their gifts and calling, the circle of friends widens and begins to move. By the grace of God, a circle of friends adds up to more than the sum of its parts.

Are you ready for action?

## EXAMPLES ARE NOT ALWAYS WHAT YOU EXPECT.

Rahab is another of those unlikely women who shows up in Matthew's genealogy of Jesus.

Rahab had a house built into the wall around Jericho, a heavily fortified city. As her story opens, Jericho happens to be the next target of the advancing Israelite army. In their quest for the land God promised them, the Israelites had already overtaken several cities, but Jericho required some strategic thinking. Joshua sent a couple of spies to get the low-down from the inside. They went to Rahab's house to stay overnight.

Did I mention Rahab's house was of ill repute? In Joshua 2, Rahab is identified as a prostitute even before we know her name. Josephus, a first-century historian known best for his history of the Jews, calls Rahab an "innkeeper." Her establishment perhaps offered both lodging for travelers and other favors for those who sought them.

Whatever her occupation, Rahab was alert to current events. She recognized these two guys as Israelites, knew Israel was in an aggressive military mode, and remembered the reputation of the God of Israel. The story of the Red Sea parting to let the Israelites leave Egypt on dry ground was in circulation, even though it was forty years old. Rahab had heard about God's promise to give the land to his people. Perhaps she had been listening to street gossip about how Jericho would defend itself. She said at one point, "No wonder our hearts have melted in fear!" so we know the street buzz was not arrogant laughter that no one could break through the walls. The mood sounded fearful that Israel would indeed succeed. It is possible Rahab had been thinking about how to align herself with the true God of Israel, and when the moment of opportunity came, she rapidly put a plan into action. There was no time to debate the ethics of her choices. She had to act fast.

The king of Jericho got wind of the two spies and ordered Rahab to produce them. Rahab lied. The truth is she stashed the spies in a pile of flax on the roof, but she told the king's men, "They left the town at dusk, as the gates were about to close. I don't know where they went. If you hurry you can probably catch up with them" (Joshua 2:5).

Having sent the king's men on a wild goose chase, Rahab dashed up to the roof to strike her deal with the Israelite spies. They owed her. She saved their lives, and now she told them what she wanted in exchange. "Swear to me by the LORD that you will be kind to me and my family since I have helped you. Give me some guarantee that when Jericho is conquered, you will let me live, along with my father and mother, my brothers and sisters, and all their families" (Joshua 2:12–13). Rahab went out on a limb when she turned away the king's men without being sure what the spies would say to her proposal. Could she trust them to keep their word? Did they even have the authority to make this promise, or did they have to go back to Joshua, Israel's leader, and persuade him to honor it? From a human perspective, she couldn't be sure how the deal would play out.

Rahab didn't say *if* Jericho is conquered, but *when*. She was confident that God was on the move, and what little she knew about God—that he is the supreme God of heaven and earth—was enough to make her want to be on his side.

The spies agree, and they make a plan that Rahab would hang a scarlet rope from the window of her house on the outside of the city wall. When the city fell, the Israelite soldiers would know to spare that house and anyone in it. Then Rahab let the spies down the wall with the scarlet rope and left it hanging. The spies gave Rahab instructions, and she followed them precisely to save both herself and her family. We read in Joshua 6 that Rahab and her family were spared when the walls of Jericho came tumbling down.

Some people read this story and get hung up on Rahab's lie. Let's not miss the point of the story. Yes, she lied. She resorted to meeting her own needs in a less than favorable way. Could she have saved the spies without doing what she did? We don't know. But the bigger picture is that God wants us to trust him, and Rahab did this. Her story is a redemption story. Through these rather odd circumstances, Rahab expressed her faith in God.

You might be taking a deep breath right about now, thinking, *If God can forgive a woman like Rahab, then there's hope for me.*

It seems to me that what God enjoys about people like Rahab is that they notice what God is doing and want to do whatever they can to get in on it. It's a dangerous deal. Rahab was an outsider, but she saw what the God of Israel was doing and was certain Jericho would fall. Her action meant risking the king's wrath if he discovered her role in hiding the spies, and it meant taking the risk of depending on the spies. Rahab took the risks because she trusted God to do what he said he was going to do. The spies were there to try to sort out how to take Jericho, as if success were up to human strategy. Rahab was confident that God was the one who would succeed.

Rahab had a long list of unworthiness, but she trusted God. Because of her willingness to risk her plan and trust in complete deliverance by the hand of God, Rahab became an ancestor of Jesus. The New Testament speaks of her faith in Hebrews 11:31 and James 2:25. She is an example for us of trusting God wholeheartedly and stepping out in action.

## TAKE THE FIRST STEP.

Carrie was a young woman who grew up in a sexually abusive environment and as a result made some poor relationship choices. Eventually she married a Christian man with a teenage daughter. Seeing God moving and working in her life through her husband drew her much closer to God as well. Carrie came to a Circle of Friends conference then joined one of our Bible study groups. After I met Carrie, I sensed the Lord telling me to invite her to join us on a ministry trip, and she went with us to Tennessee. She turned out to be a huge help and became involved in our ministry. We once received the gift of free space at a conference that otherwise would have cost thousands of ministry dollars to participate in. Carrie and another friend went along to work the table. The two of them would engage with people who stopped by to find out more about Circle of Friends. They were looking for a way to encourage other women but were not sure what that would look like.

"Just be kind," I said, encouraging the encouragers. "Offer to pray if someone looks like she's hurting. Believe what you've learned the last six months, and God will help you."

Carrie talked to people from all over and eagerly prayed. She took a risk and stepped out into action and discovered a whole new dimension to her own ministry.

I met another woman at a conference who seemed burdened.

"How are you today?" I asked.

"Not so good," came the answer.

"Everything all right at home?"

"No."

"Want to talk?"

It was as if she was just waiting for someone to ask. She had been widowed and had raised a son, who was now a teenager. Married again to a pastor, recently she had lost a baby through miscarriage. The weight of her grief was palpable, but I sensed there was something more.

"I thought the miscarriage would make us closer," she said, "then last weekend my husband told me he's gay. He said he wants to work through this and doesn't want to split up, but he said I can't talk to anyone at church. I have to find someone else."

She had come by herself to the conference, looking for an opportunity to speak a painful truth from her life. I invited her to dinner with a group of friends. We did not have further conversation about the challenge she faced, but just being in the presence of someone who knew the truth seemed to restore her spirit. She had risked the first step.

## What will you risk?

Rahab got out of her comfort zone and dealt with a bad situation with an uncertain outcome. Carrie got out of her comfort zone and began a ministry that made her nervous at first. The woman I met at the conference stepped out of her comfort zone and said aloud words she never expected to speak.

Getting out of your comfort zone—isn't that the heart of taking a risk? If you could be sure of the outcome, you wouldn't be uncomfortable. But if you don't take the risk, you may also miss out on seeing how God is moving.

Some of our comfort zones are cozy, comfy couches. We're so comfortable, there seems to be no reason to get up. Ever. Life is good. Happy stuff happens on that comfy couch. Good friends, family, work—it's all good.

Some of our comfort zones are hard, bruising places. What makes them comfortable is that at least we know what to expect. It may not be a Hallmark card kind of life, but at least it's familiar. We know how things work in that zone.

Getting out of the comfort zone means letting go. We might have to let go of the things that made us feel safe. We might have to let go of the things that are familiar, even if they are not safe. Like Rahab, we have to take a risk and trust God.

How many times have you said, "I know I need to trust God, but. . ." Finish the sentence with whatever you are holding on to. There's always an unknown, something we can't control, something we can't be sure of. If we have to be sure of everything in order to trust, that's not really trust.

What did Rahab put her trust in? She trusted God because she saw him moving. She saw that God had a plan for his people and he was keeping his word to them. She saw that she had an opportunity to be part of what God was doing. She saw that this God of Israel was the one true God. Although the battle was still ahead and the outcome was uncertain, everything she believed to be true pointed her toward God, and when the moment came, she stepped out of her comfort zone and into action.

Where is your comfort zone? What is so familiar to you that it feels like your own skin—even if it's not good for you? What might God be asking you to let go of so that you can step into the adventure he has planned for your life? Rahab's moment came, and she answered the call. What is your moment?

Getting out of the comfort zone is the adventure of a lifetime. It reminds me of looking at mountains and wondering how to cross them to discover the land waiting on the other side. Imagine what the pioneers went through when they crossed the Rockies. It's not going to be easy, but it's worth the risk because of what awaits us on the other side. We move out of the wilderness of slavery to fear and loneliness and into new life. If we don't take the first step up the mountain, we don't move into the promised land.

> *The ladies of Circle of Friends delight in helping others discover what their gifts and talents might be. Encouragement is such a high priority. I am talking about encouragement that is not flattery, but is given for the purpose of building up women and instilling Christ-centered confidence in them to develop areas in their lives previously neglected or undiscovered. Circle of Friends lovingly comes alongside people to spur them on to become what God created them to be and do. —Libby*

Our society is driven by instantaneous results, but that's not reality. Moving out of the comfort zone involves pain just as any other exercise or discipline does. The flesh says, *This is not worth it. I hate it.* But when you hit your stride, you wonder how you ever lived without it.

You have to take a risk. The first attempt at a relationship of accountability or some new dimension of ministry may not be successful. It's not a failure if it doesn't work out the first time. Failure is never being willing to attempt something. If we don't take risks, the world remains very small.

I understand that taking risks can be frightening, especially for people who have been abused or wounded or deeply disappointed in the past. It feels like standing around on the playground waiting to see if a team captain is going to pick you or if you'll be the one nobody wants on the team. But even if you are the last person chosen for the team, if you put what God has given you into action, others may be surprised at what happens.

In the next few chapters, you'll find some inspiring stories about people who stepped out of their comfort zones as part of the Circle of Friends ministry. You'll also find some resources to help you step out of yours. It's time for action!

# 25

# YOUR HEART AND GOD'S HEART

*Transformation begins on the inside.*

God wants to move in your life. I am 100 percent sure of that. God wants you to discover the purpose and meaning that he gives to your life. God wants you to get out of your comfort zone and into an action mode. I know you have questions.

*How do I know if this is God speaking or just human emotion?*

*How can I learn to listen to God better?*

*How can I get closer to God when I hardly have time to breathe?*

*I can't remember what I ate for lunch, so how can I keep track of what God is saying to me?*

All good questions! God created people with a wide variety of temperaments and personalities, so we don't all get close to God in the same way. An outgoing person may get the best spiritual insights or ministry ideas through stimulating conversation with other people. A quieter person may prefer to be alone to find a way to block out the noise of life and listen for God's still small voice. No one way of encountering God is the "right" way, but we all need to attend to the inner life and open our hearts to how God moves in and through us. We come to God first of all in worship. We acknowledge him to be the Lord and display our humility in his presence. And then we are ready to listen to what he wants to say to us.

Many people find keeping a journal to be helpful. Your first response might be that a journal is fine for bookworms with time on their hands, but that doesn't describe you or your life. But just as there is no one right way of encountering God, there is no one right way to keep a journal. It's a tool, so each person learns to use it in a way that benefits her.

## PLOW WITH YOUR JOURNAL.

If a journal is a tool, what do we use it for? The Old Testament prophet Jeremiah reminds us that God said to his people, "Plow up the hard ground of your hearts!" (Jeremiah 4:3). Journaling helps to clear away whatever may be keeping you from knowing God's presence and seeing God's movement in your life.

Here are some ideas for how this tool plows the hard ground.

**A journal is a safe place.** In a journal, you can be honest with God and honest with yourself. It's okay to say you're mad at your husband or fed up with your coworker or exasperated with your neighbor. It's okay to say that you are overwhelmed with life and not sure you can get out of bed tomorrow. It's okay to face a decision and be confused about what is the right choice

One of the things I love about the Psalms in the Bible is that they are full of raw life. David, the great king of Israel and a man after God's own heart, lets loose with how he really feels. We never have to wonder what he thinks about his enemies! We hear his questions about where God is in a troubling situation. But we also hear his confession and praise as his eyes turn back to the Lord in worship and he finds solace and strength.

In a journal, you write the psalms of your own life. You can say, "I'm angry at. . . ," or "I'm frustrated because. . . ," or "I'm totally confused," or "Lord, speak to me." You can say what your life is without feeling like you have to clean it up for anyone else. Put real life on the page and see what God is going to do with it.

**A journal is a process.** You might feel emotional pain when you begin to write and release by the time you put your pen down. You might feel bewildered when you begin but be clear on the next step to take when you close your notebook. You might begin with questions and find the answers in your own words.

The point of a journal is not just to write down the raw elements of life to justify your shortcomings. It's not to avoid screaming at somebody else because you got your frustration out of your system on paper, as beneficial as that may be. Rather, journaling is a process. You begin at one point and open your heart to where the words may take you. If a neighbor's needs are on your heart but you don't see how you can help, you might be surprised at the insights that come when you pause long enough to give the question some mental energy. If you're considering a new commitment but feel unsure if it's the right thing to do, writing your way through the issues might well bring clarity to the decision.

Not every question is solved in one twenty-minute session of journaling. Writing about something that's on your mind might open the door of your heart to understanding the real questions, and you may return to them repeatedly over a period of time. That's all part of the process.

The process of journaling may spark ideas, clear confusion, or help you hear God speak to you on a particular subject. Rather than being a retreat from life, journaling intersects real life and points you in a direction for action.

**A journal is a record.** Some people keep journals for years, piling up spiral upon spiral notebook. If you use this tool over a long period of time, you create a record of your own spiritual journey. No one else takes the same journey you do. No one else learns exactly the same lessons that you do.

The lessons you learn are first of all for you. When you look over the record of your journey, you can see change. You can see your starting points on various issues and also your ending points. Periodically looking through old journals may prompt you to remember some of the paths you've taken and how your connection to God deepened because of these experiences. Perhaps reviewing old lessons will offer fresh encouragement in a new stage of life.

The lessons you learn may also be for others. Perhaps you've lived through an experience in a way that allows you to offer encouragement to another woman going through something similar. Your interactions with scripture, recorded in a journal, may provide the framework for teaching others these lessons from God's Word.

A record invites you to look at the big picture. It's like tracing your family tree back four hundred years. Most of the time we are consumed with our own generation, or perhaps the generation that comes just before or just after us. But if we have the opportunity to trace our ancestors, we get a bigger sense of where we came from and how we got to be us. The record of a journal is like that—it reminds you of where you came from and what brought you to the life you have right now. You can trace the hand of God in your life and get the picture of what he is growing in you.

## MASTER THE TOOL.

Whenever we pick up a new tool, we have to get the feel of it, try it out, and gradually master how to use it effectively. The same is true of a journal. Here are some ideas that might help.

**Make a habit.** Journaling can be like a New Year's resolution to go to the gym. Lots of people talk about it, but talking about it doesn't make it happen. *Doing* is what matters.

Habits take about three weeks to form, and they depend on specific behaviors. What behaviors does journaling require?

- What kind of notebook will you write in?
- Will you choose a physical location for entering the journaling zone?
- What time of day is realistic for your schedule?
- How often will you journal? Daily? Three times a week? Once a week?
- How long will you write? Five minutes? Ten? Thirty?

I can't tell you the right answers, and it doesn't work to try to copy someone else's method. No one else has your life. If you want to begin journaling, think through how it can really work in your life.

**Write what comes to mind.** Don't worry about writing something profound. You don't have to have a fully formed thought to begin moving your pen across the page. Remember, journaling is a process that will shed light on what puzzles you. You're not writing for publication; you're writing as a way to draw closer to God.

**Keep a Bible handy.** Some people like to organize their journals around reflecting on specific passages from the Bible. Others like to copy an occasional verse that encourages or challenges them. You may find yourself somewhere in between. However, because journaling draws you into a deeper spiritual walk, God's Spirit may prompt you to reach for your Bible and take you to a specific passage. When you pick up your journal, pick up a Bible as well.

**Pray.** Offer your journaling time to God, and ask him to speak to you. You may simply want to pray before you begin, or you may want to consciously write a prayer that begins or ends your journaling session.

A woman named Sharon says about her journals, "I journal every morning and do my daily reading. I have years of journals. I don't know when I will read them, but I need to write them. I love my mornings with God and a couple of cups of Caribou coffee." Sharon's life hasn't been easy, and a deep relationship with Jesus is a relatively new experience for her. For Sharon, journaling helps to plow up the hard ground of her heart and point her toward where God leads. Having suffered the pain of divorce more than once, Sharon now says, "Jesus is my husband. I know God has a plan."

> *My pastor asked if they could give out my name to a divorced woman to meet with her, listen, and help her if I was able. I never would have thought I could help anyone. But if I don't step out and share my story, it will have been in vain. I look back at what God has done in me, and I am shocked! The person I was is dead. I am a new creation. I only want to live to praise him. —Sharon*

In my spiritual life, I joyfully recall those "holy dot" moments—transformational times when God, through his kindness, led me to repentance. God moves me from point A to point B to point C, connecting the dots of the events of my life until the picture emerges.

I pray you will step into your journey with God. As you seek the ministry God is preparing you for, look inside. Let God prepare your heart so that when the opportunity comes to take action, you will be ready.

# 26

# AVAILABLE AND OBEDIENT

*God orchestrates the outcome.*

I knew God called me into women's ministry on a June day in 1998. I remember feeling a sense of direction and purpose I'd never felt before that Sunday afternoon. I felt so thrilled that it was okay that I had not been perfect up to that point in my life. God would transform my imperfection and give me purpose beyond the ministries of being a wife and a mom. Those are high callings, and I'm privileged to be married to Bob and to be Jillian and Christian's mom. But God also had a mission for me to entreat other women to see God as the person who will go out of his way to meet with them and tell them everything they'd ever done—and love them anyway.

God challenges us to recognize the factors in our lives that cause us to remain isolated. Sometimes we look at other women who seem to have more fulfilling lives than we do and wonder, *Will I ever be able to be part of something, or am I destined to always be by myself because of the shame of my past?* A lot of us are socially interactive but spiritually alone. We're with other people but not saying the things we need to say about what's really going on. When we go to the well and meet Jesus, we can have our spiritual dryness filled up. We don't have to live with shame and insecurity coloring everything we do.

I knew that this was the heart of the message I could share with other women, but I had no idea what this women's ministry would look like. This was the beginning of Circle of Friends, but the ministry unfolded over the years—and continues to unfold. God brought key people to our circle. I've sometimes been flabbergasted at the opportunities that come to us, but our attitude is to be available and obedient to God's movement in our work.

## GOD BRINGS PEOPLE TO YOUR CIRCLE.

I've mentioned my good friend Beth a couple of times. I first met her through a chain of circumstances that made it clear God was putting us together. I once gave a copy of *The Message* translation of the New Testament to one seventh grader I thought would appreciate it. He lay on a trampoline and read avidly, later telling me how much he enjoyed having it. After hearing his account, the thought emerged, *Wouldn't it be great if every seventh grader in the school district could obtain one, free upon request?*

I took that challenge to my Bible study group. We decided to put an ad in the newspaper with a safe e-mail address, and anyone who wanted a free Bible for a seventh grader could respond. Beth's daughter was going into seventh grade, and Beth responded to the ad. We sent her a New Testament for her daughter. Beth had that copy of the New Testament with her one day in church, and a woman from my group recognized it and said, "I know where you got that." She told Beth about our group. Shortly after that, I got an e-mail from Beth that said, "Hello, Lisa. Now I know who this is." We began a relationship, and later Beth said to me, "I feel like I'm supposed to ask you to lead worship at our women's retreat." We were not attending the same church at the time. Both of us were home with young children, involved in women's groups, and hungry for the Lord. It didn't take us long to learn that we both had been rowdy teenagers, and we helped each other work through the regrets we had. Together we recognized that what happened to us when we were young skewed our thinking about how God feels about us.

The upshot is that Beth has been with me since the early days of Circle of Friends. When I gave that first Bible to one seventh-grade boy for a birthday present, I had no idea what it would lead to. But whatever happened, I wanted to be open and available.

## God has vast imagination for you.

I've mentioned my friend Andrea a couple of times, too. She's a fantastic Bible teacher. She once was offered the opportunity to record a couple of studies to air on a local radio station. The general manager was interested to see what might happen with such a program. As exciting as the opportunity was, Andrea felt that she was to wait, so she declined. Because she made that decision out of obedience, I ended up in conversation with the general manager, who offered me the opportunity to do an evening radio program. I could be live one night a week and record the other shows. My husband's response to the opportunity was, "Duh. You've been praying for an opportunity to minister to women in the community." With his encouragement, I accepted the offer. I interviewed singer Sheila Walsh on the first show. The program emphasized real conversation about real-life issues. Sheila shared openly about her own experience with clinical depression. The show gained listeners quickly, and within two years this program broadcast from a small Christian station had the same ratings as a top show at a secular counterpart station.

When Circle of Friends launched, we didn't list as one of our goals, "Develop radio personality." Yet that is exactly the direction God led us. The program I began hosting at night transformed into a midday program hosted by a panel of women from Circle of Friends.

Later when Garry Meeks, the manager at the station in Canton, heard that Family Life Radio in Tucson, Arizona, was looking for a host for a women's program, he thought I should record a demo and send it to them. First I got sick and could not make the recording. Then the equipment went on the blink, with just two days till the deadline. In the end, I couldn't make a new demo, but I did send a recording of our local program.

I was extremely surprised when the producer in Tucson called back and said they wanted to pair me with another woman from Los Angeles to record a pilot show. However, the proposed date conflicted with my daughter's Christmas program. I assumed that because I was unavailable, the opportunity would pass with a "Sorry, we can't change the schedule," but they graciously delayed the recording. The night before I was supposed to fly, though, a horrible snowstorm hit the area where I live. I wasn't even sure I could get to the airport, much less whether the plane could get in the air. In the end, everything worked out, and we recorded the pilot. Now I was waiting to hear where this might lead. A few weeks later, though, the network took on a new program director, and nothing came of the pilot.

It seemed like a dead end, but I was content because I had simply tried to be available and obedient. However, because of that demo, Dick Lee, station manager at Moody Radio Cleveland who had previously worked for Family Life Network, expressed interest. He listened to the demo I had prepared for Tucson and offered me the opportunity to do a regular program on the Moody affiliate. I'm still doing that program. I aim my content at a female audience, but men started listening as well. People are responding to authentic conversation about what life is like and what God is doing.

Once again, God orchestrated a different outcome than what I imagined. Every time he does that, I am again encouraged to keep myself available and obedient to what God wants to do. We look for ministry opportunities, but sometimes they come to us in such clear ways that we can have no doubt that God is making the arrangements.

## SHARE THE FEAST.

We don't always understand how our bodies break down fruits and vegetables, but they do, and it's good for us. It's the same with God's Word. When we take it in, it does something good for us. Steeping ourselves in God's Word was at the heart of the initial accountability group I was in with Beth and Andrea. Andrea was direct: Make time! We started using the *One Year Bible* that arranged Bible portions into daily readings. If you keep up with the daily readings, in a year's time you read the entire Bible. Rather than reading straight through from Genesis to Revelation, a one-year plan offers daily readings from the Old Testament, the New Testament, Psalms, and Proverbs. Each day's readings are laid out so you don't have to worry about flipping pages and looking for passages. Other editions arrange passages in a chronological order, rather than the order that books appear in the Bible, so the reader has more of a sense of reading one overarching story.

This experience changed our lives, and as Circle of Friends grew, we decided to offer the *One Year Bible* to all the participants who come to our conferences. We want other women to have the same rich feast of God's Word that we had. If you prefer to read from your own familiar Bible, a one-year reading plan gives you the same opportunity to immerse yourself in God's Word. (You'll find a daily Bible reading plan in the Resources section of this book.)

Something as simple as sharing the experience of reading God's Word became a catalyst for ministry. Ministry doesn't always have to be involved and complicated. Sometimes it is just saying, "This made a difference for me. I hope it will make a difference for you, too."

## God will surprise you.

In 2009 I headed to Cleveland to co-host the Moody Women's Conference at Parkside Church, sponsored by the radio station I work for. I had no idea what God had planned for me. One of the speakers was Virelle Kidder, a vivacious woman with a sweet smile who put me in mind of my late aunt Alice, right down to the flashy glasses. I looked forward to what she would have to say.

As one of the hosts of the conference, it was my job to share with the audience the subject that Virelle would present. I received a card with a bit of introductory information. Little did I know that Virelle had written a book called *Meet Me at the Well*. My antennae went straight up. The story of the Samaritan woman at the well in John 4 was the launching point for my calling into women's ministry and the beginning of Circle of Friends. I sat there captivated, somewhat in disbelief, as Virelle shared from her heart what easily could have been phrases and feelings I journaled a decade before. Mixed in with her illustrations from John 4 was her transparency about her own faith journey.

God used Virelle's invitation at the end of the conference to usher several women into a personal relationship with Jesus. Afterward, a number of women crowded around Virelle for further conversation. I needed to get home to my family, so I said a brief good-bye to Virelle and asked if I could contact her.

A few days later, I sent her an e-mail. I wanted to invite her to be a guest either on my program on the Moody network or on the Circle of Friends radio program. I also told her that the material in her book would be a great catalyst for songs relating to women and the needs in our lives.

Virelle's e-mail reply indicated that she wanted to talk about this music idea. We spoke on the phone for more than an hour getting to know one another and exploring the idea of developing a CD that would be a companion to her book. One thing led to another as God put the pieces together. I had contacts in Nashville, and a simple query by e-mail turned into meetings with musicians and producers. Not everything went according to schedule— except it went according to God's plan. Schedule conflicts and changed plans led to last-minute opportunities, and the right people came into the pic-ture to create the *Meet Me at the Well* album. Virelle and I have had the privilege of ministering together around this theme that changed our lives because God brought us together at that conference.

> *The first time I heard Lisa perform the amazing songs on her Meet Me at the Well album, I was stunned by her captivating voice, her unaffected talent, her heart for ministry. We were in a large crowd of women in New England, and all over the room women were weeping. Yes, God was in it for sure. As I reflect upon the early events of our relationship, I marvel at what God has done. Not only has God given us a precious friendship, but so much proceeded from that first meeting that it makes my head spin. What will God do next? I have no idea, but I can hardly wait. —Virelle Kidder*

## GOD IS RIGHT THERE.

I've certainly had some unique opportunities, and so has the ministry of Circle of Friends. Relationships of acceptance, authenticity, affirmation, and accountability have led to stepping out in action. We've made ourselves available to the opportunities that God sometimes plunks down in the middle of our unsuspecting lives.

Mary, the mother of Jesus, is a wonderful example of making herself available and obedient to God. Luke tells her story in chapter 1 of his gospel.

Most likely a teenager, Mary was living a quiet life in the village of Nazareth when one day the angel Gabriel appeared to her and said, "Greetings, favored woman. The Lord is with you."

Luke tells us Mary was "confused and disturbed" and "tried to think what the angel could mean" (Luke 1:29). No doubt seeing the confusion in the girl's face, the angel obliged with more explanation. He told her that God had chosen her to be the mother of his Son. Her baby would sit on the throne of David and reign over Israel.

As amazing as this sounds, it didn't exactly clear everything up in Mary's mind. The question Mary voiced aloud was, "How can this happen?" But we can well imagine she's thinking. *What will Joseph think? My parents will never believe this. Nobody in the village will speak to me if I turn up pregnant before my wedding.*

> *This is a group of ladies on the move! God is at work in and through Circle of Friends. When I listen to them during the day, I know I will learn something, find a kindred spirit, and feel closer to God. —Ellenjean*

Gabriel answered the question Mary asked. The Holy Spirit would be at work, he told her. That is how she would conceive a child. And just in case Mary still had doubts, the angel informed her that her relative Elizabeth was also pregnant—six months along. Elizabeth was way past childbearing age and never had a child before, but she was having one now. After all, nothing is impossible with God.

Perhaps the news about Elizabeth made Mary's breath catch. Perhaps it was the angel's reminder that nothing is impossible with God. Despite her questions and confusion, Mary now accepted the mission and made herself available.

"I am the Lord's servant," she said, "May everything you have said about me come true" (Luke 1:38).

Mary chose to be available and obedient. She had a glimpse of what God was doing and wanted to step in and be a part of it. That's what taking action is all about. She still had to face her parents and Joseph and the village, but she was certain that God was in the middle of it all.

As you consider the risks God may ask you to take and how he is preparing and transforming you to take them, you don't have to look far. Don't make stepping out in action more complicated than it has to be. God is right there with you, and while your eyes are focused on something off in the distance, God may be waving an opportunity right in front of your face. Blink your eyes and refocus.

What circumstances in your life seem to have the fingerprint of God on them?

What might change if you adopt an attitude of availability to God?

What could happen if you look at what's around you and ask the question, "What if . . . ?"

Don't miss the blessing of being available and obedient to step into action in your spiritual journey.

# 27

# GIRLFRIENDS AND MORE

*Start with what matters most to you.*

**M**y good friend Beth has five—count 'em, *five*—children. So it's easy to understand why she cares about the moments when kids make choices that can change their lives.

Beth and a friend, Denise, had girls in the same class. One of their daughters' friends made a poor decision that spurred Beth and Denise into action. The girl talked to a complete stranger hanging around the playground on a Saturday. Beth and Denise were alarmed. Nothing happened at that point, but the girl continued to make choices that concerned them, and they knew her choices had the potential to haunt her for years. Together they decided to launch a program in a group setting where someone would talk about how choices impact not only our own lives, but our friends' as well.

Becki's only daughter, Liz, was murdered. Liz had a friend who decided to give a stranger a ride in exchange for gas money. That choice, made in a split second, had rippling consequences that changed the lives of many people forever. Now Becki talks to other girls about the choices they make as part of the ministry Beth and Denise launched.

## GET STARTED AND SEE WHERE IT GOES.

The program Beth and Denise launched is called Girlfriends. It's an annual event they offer to seventh grade girls in their school district. Becki talks about what happened to her daughter. A police officer talks about pedophiles and Internet sex crimes. They also pull in a college-age man to answer questions about what guys really think. Girls ask point-blank questions. Speakers tell hard truth. It's not just a couple of moms telling kids to be careful. They bring in the ugly realities of what could happen and talk to kids who are at an age when they are making more and more independent choices every day. Then they balance that with a lighter note and invite a clothing or image stylist to talk to the girls, or bring in hair and beauty college graduates. Girls can explore modesty and hair and makeup as a way to make choices that will impact their lives for the good in the years to come.

Moms are invited to attend with their daughters, and many do come and find out what it's all about. Beth and Denise warn the mothers that the program is hard-hitting. They don't shy away from death, murder, and gruesome themes. The girls' faces when they hear Becki talk about her daughter is evidence that the program is getting through. Kids may or may not listen to their parents, but when they hear someone else say the same things their parents say, they listen twice as hard.

Girlfriends has grown into other events. A May event for seventh and eighth graders tackles the theme of dating. A ninth-grade Girls Night Out aims at girls who are not allowed to date or don't get asked to the homecoming dance. A woman named Rebecca with a bistro opens her establishment for a gourmet meal, and college girls come in and serve the high schoolers. After the meal, where the girls are treated like princesses, they go to the dance together. In another event becoming a tradition, a local doctor opens a building known as "the barn" for girls in tenth through twelfth grades to enjoy a movie and popcorn night.

The original seventh graders enjoy each new event as they get older, but more important, they enjoy relationships with adults who care about them. By getting involved with other people's daughters, Beth and Denise become adult faces the girls can connect with even outside of church or school. They are one more person to speak encouragement and truth into the lives of the girls as they go through their teen years. The girls also get to know each other outside a school setting and form stronger relationships to support each other. Moms get connected with each other. Moms and daughters get talking to each other about things they might not have ventured into on their own.

The Girlfriends program would be easy to replicate. It just takes a couple of moms to do the groundwork that makes it happen. Maybe you're already thinking of the girls you could invite to an event like this.

## WATCH FOR THE NEXT OPPORTUNITY.

Just as a good sitcom often has spin-offs, so does a strong ministry. One of the moms connected to Girlfriends wanted to pray for children at a local elementary school. She did not just want to pray for the students who attend; she wanted to pray *at* the school. She got the necessary permission and organized a group of moms to pray for students at the school, for the adults who have influence in their lives, for their teachers, for the school board.

A man who lived in a retirement community got wind of the prayer group and asked if he could join. This evolved into meeting with retirees in their community to pray for kids in school. This happens twice a month on Thursday morning. The group prays for the children in their local school and also for children in schools across the nation. One man said, "There's so much I can't do anymore, but I can still pray."

Can you launch a Girlfriends ministry where you live? Can you organize a prayer team? Can you (_____)? Girlfriends started because two moms cared about something specific—preparing adolescent girls to

*I found a place to belong at the first annual Circle of Friends conference. God placed me at my job in the church where the conference was being held, and I just happened to be the contact person for the conference. I discovered the love and fellowship I craved with the women at Circle of Friends. I am honored and excited to continue to be a part of this group in many wonderful ways, and am amazed at just how our circle is expanding. It is so exciting to see how God is using this group of God-loving, God-serving women to bring hope to women around the world. —Becki*

make good choices. The prayer ministry spun off of that. Both of these ideas could be duplicated in virtually any community in the country. But even more, the model of how they began can be duplicated: somebody cared and did something about it. It's that simple.

What is something on your heart that really matters to you? That may be the starting point for the ministry God has in mind for you. What can you do in your neighborhood that would touch lives of individual people? How can you get involved with your school district, or how might your church be a resource for a ministry that touches the community? What's on your heart might even be a need on the other side of the world, but you may be in a position to lead others near you in providing resources that changes lives of people you'll never meet.

As you answer God's call to step out into action and walk in his purpose for your life, think about what tugs at your heart. Start there.

# 28

# WHO, ME? A LEADER?

*Grow in your ministry.*

S tepping out in action requires taking risks, because we cannot be certain
of the outcome.

*If I step out in friendship, will someone respond?*

*If I step out in hospitality, will someone feel welcome?*

*If I step out in Bible study, will others want to learn with me?*

*If I step out in transparency, will others respond with kindness?*

*If I step out with the truth, with anyone still talk to me?*

*If I step out in ministry, will it make any difference?*

It's certainly easy to think "Probably not" as an answer to questions like
these and quickly talk ourselves out of even trying. It's not worth the effort,
we think. It's not worth the risk.

This is where we have to remind ourselves that the real question is
not what others will do, but how we ourselves are responding to the ways
God nudges us. Are we staying close enough to God to hear his voice and
trace his fingerprint? Are we making ourselves available to God's surprise
opportunities? Are we letting our hearts find the things we really care about?

God asks all of us for attitudes of worship and availability. The action
God calls us to differs from person to person. Our God-given personality
types equip us for a range of ministries, and a circle of friends is wide enough
to celebrate the diversity of gifts. God may even be calling some of you to
step into action as leader of your own circle of friends.

# Where do I start?

Here's a possible starting point: Five Friends, Five Weeks.

• Find four friends and form a group of five. Consider inviting some women you don't know well along with some you do.

• Commit to meet together once a week for five weeks. You don't need a fancy or official place. You can gather around the kitchen table or grab a space at your favorite coffee shop. Stress that this is a short-term commitment for just five meetings.

• During each meeting, talk about one of the five themes of this book—acceptance, authenticity, affirmation, accountability, action. At the end of this chapter, you'll find discussion guides for these five sessions. No one is the teacher, and there are no right or wrong answers. Use a round table format where every person can speak without judgment.

Provide a copy of the discussion guide for each person. Begin by reading aloud the paragraphs that present the theme. Encourage everyone to underline words or phrases that stand out. Once you finish reading, look at the discussion questions together. Begin by inviting others to share what they underlined and why particular phrases stuck out to them. Continue with the remaining questions. Not everyone has to answer every question, but it's important that each woman has a chance to contribute to the discussion.

Five friends, five weeks, five themes. It's a simple start.

At the end of these five meetings, talk about what the women in the group might like to do next. Remember, not everyone may decide to stay with the group. Be gracious toward anyone who feels she cannot continue, for whatever reason. For those who would like to continue, the possibilities are wide open.

Your group might decide to begin a structured Bible study. You can use prepared materials available from a variety of publishers, or perhaps you know someone who might enjoy teaching a Bible study group if you asked.

Your group might decide to continue in a round table format. LaRed is an organization that offers free resources for groups using a round table format. The premise of their work is that values bring powerful change. They offer forty faith-based values from the book of Proverbs with a short article you can print easily and brief discussion questions for each theme.

You can explore practical applications of themes such as patience, restraint, temper, responsibility, listening, and more. Go to www.lared.org for more information.

Your group may even decide that you would like to go deeper into relationships of authenticity and accountability. In the Resources section of this book, you'll find a list of accountability questions that can serve as the backbone of your conversations as you get started. Later you might like to customize the list of questions for your own group.

Your group may decide to step out into action together with a particular ministry or service project. You'll get to know each other more deeply as you serve side by side.

The key principle is that you do not have to know the ending point in order to get started. Simply begin with five friends, five weeks, and five themes. Let God lead you to the next step.

## CONNECT YOUR CIRCLE OF FRIENDS TO OURS.

Circle of Friends Ministries has an annual conference in Ohio. If you can come, great! We'd love to have you. But that is not the only way to connect with us. Feel free to contact us directly through our website, www.ourcircleoffriends.org, with questions about starting your own circle of friends, or special needs on your heart. On the website you'll also find a blog with multiple contributors and daily devotional readings. If you think you would like to contribute to the devotionals, check out the writer's guidelines. You can listen to Circle of Friends radio ministry anytime by clicking the link on the website, including music and panel discussions. We invite you to connect with us in whatever ways will encourage and inspire you. As you step out into action in your own circle of friends, let us circle around you any way we can.

# FIVE FRIENDS, FIVE WEEKS
# DISCUSSION GUIDES

# THEME 1: ACCEPTANCE

*We welcome you to embark on an adventure in relationship. Come as you are:*

Finding a place to belong—where people notice you and care—begins with accepting that God notices you and cares. This is the start of realizing you don't have to go it alone. We need each other. You do not have to present an invincible front to the world. You don't have to hold things together so that no one sees what you are really like. Your circle of friends can come around you in a time of need. And in acceptance you can rally around the friend who feels that she is stretched too thin or that what she holds inside herself is too fragile for public display.

You matter to God, and you matter to other people. Imagine what life could be like if you told just one person your deepest ache. Imagine talking freely about your faith questions and puzzling decisions and life dreams. We need each other to reflect on the road behind us and ponder what lies ahead. As companions on the journey, we help each other see God's truth rather than our own fears. The journey begins in relationships of acceptance, and those relationships are rooted in God's love for each one of us.

*1. What parts of these paragraphs speak to you most? If you can, explain why.*

*2. What is one of the hardest things about admitting that you need other people?*

*3. Tell about an experience of feeling accepted. Tell about an experience of not feeling accepted.*

*4. How does feeling accepted make it easier to speak honestly?*

*5. What is the connection between knowing that God accepts you and being able to accept others?*

# THEME 2: AUTHENTICITY

*We invite you to exchange the familiar for the extraordinary. It's worth the risk.*

God wants you to be real, and in being real—in an intimate relationship with him just as you are—you see where you belong. We all have watershed moments with the potential to change everything. How we respond to them can alter the stories of our lives. Will we recognize the important moments in our lives and hear God's voice calling in the midst of them? Will we respond by pretending to hold it all together, or will we respond by helping each other face truth? We don't have to let shame or fear determine our lives. As unhealthy as the patterns of our lives may be, they become familiar. When we let pretending die, we exchange the familiar for something extraordinary.

We can't have a well-rounded life without real relationships. We need people who encourage us to take risks. We need to be people who encourage others to risk authenticity. God never meant for us to be alone. Relationships based on truth and love—not pretending or trying to measure up—can change us.

Let's risk being real with God. Let's risk being real with one other person. That's a good starting point. Let's not be afraid of the friends we could become.

*1. What parts of these paragraphs speak to you most? If you can, explain why.*

*2. Describe the difference between being real and not being real.*

*3. What keeps us from being authentic in friendship?*

*4. What is the role of friendship in being real?*

*5. Is it easier to be real with God or to be real with another person?*

# THEME 3: AFFIRMATION

*We dare you to enrich the lives of those around you. No one else is you.*

Being real with God opens us up to a new kind of living, and being real with other people allows us to enter their lives. Now we journey together in the light rather than alone in shadows.

Nobody's perfect. We all have our reasons for feeling like we're a hindrance to other people, but we fall back on the faithful character of God. As sordid as our lives may be, nothing is beyond God's redemptive power. No matter what our circumstances, God can make something significant and beautiful out of our lives. God wants to use us right where we are in the context of our ordinary lives. Part of being real with each other is helping one another discover and use the gifts that make each of us unique. That's the heart of affirmation. Let's not limit God by settling for limitations.

Who are the people God brings across our paths? What we give to others is in direct correlation to what God has done in our hearts and lives. Let's grab hold of the gifts God puts at our disposal, even if they seem to come in unexpected and outlandish ways. Let's step into our gifts.

*1. What parts of these paragraphs speak to you most? If you can, explain why.*



*2. What is the difference between affirmation and flattery?*



*3. Name some ways that friends can affirm each other's gifts.*

*4. How do you tend to respond when someone affirms your gifts?*


*5. What might hold us back from discovering and using our gifts?*

# THEME 4: ACCOUNTABILITY

*We encourage you to receive the comfort of companionship. Be set free!*

Relationships of acceptance, authenticity, and affirmation make it safe to have relationships of accountability. When we find a place to belong, we can see the beauty in our own scars because of what God is doing in our lives, even if the process is painful. We can move through the hard places and come out on the other end with a stronger relationship with the Lord. God accepts us as we are and invites us into an adventure of relationship. God's vision for our lives challenges us to risk exchanging the familiar for the extraordinary. God gives us gifts to enrich the lives of those around us. As we go deeper into relationships with God and others, we discover the freedom that comes from telling the truth.

Accountability is an experience of love, not judgment, and it will keep you growing spiritually through the busyness and challenges of your life. We can learn from our mistakes and be set free by the truth. Accountability is companionship on the journey into a transforming life with God. We don't get any extra credit for trying to figure things out on our own, rather than hearing the counsel of people who know us well. We need people who keep us at the feet of Jesus, learning from him.

*1. What parts of these paragraphs speak to you most? If you can, explain why.*

*2. For you personally, what's the scariest part of being accountable to another person?*

3. If accountability is mutual, rather than authoritarian, what difference does that make?

4. How have other people in your life helped you learn from Jesus?

5. When we face challenges, what might make us prefer to be on our own, rather than in relationships with other people?

# Theme 5: Action

*We pray you will step into your journey. Walk in your purpose.*

Acceptance, authenticity, affirmation, and accountability make us bold to step out in action. By the grace of God, a circle of friends adds up to more than the sum of its parts. As we seek the ministry God is preparing us for, we look inside and let God prepare our hearts so that when the opportunity comes to take action, we will be ready. God asks us to be available and obedient, and he will orchestrate the outcome. Sometimes he surprises us with his vast imagination!

Something that really matters to us may be the starting point for the ministry God has in mind. Other opportunities may spin off of that. Answering God's call and walking in the purpose he has for us may be as simple as recognizing what tugs at our hearts.

Finding a place to belong is not just to give us a comfortable place to hang out. A circle of friends is not about making life easier, but about making it richer and more full of the joy and meaning that comes from the ways we touch each other's lives. It's time to step out of our comfort zones and into God's adventure.

*1. What parts of these paragraphs speak to you most? If you can, explain why.*

*2. Name some reasons we fall into comfort zones.*

*3. For you personally, what is the hardest part of getting out of a comfort zone?*

*4. What tugs at your heart at this season of your life?*

*5. What risks are involved in being available and obedient to God?*

# 29

# WHAT ARE YOU WAITING FOR?

*Where will you begin?*

I warned you that I would keep saying that finding a place to belong is not just to give you a comfortable place to hang out. So I'm saying it again. Your circle of friends is not about making your life easier, but about making it richer and more full of the joy and meaning that come from the ways we touch each other's lives. It's about getting you out of your comfort zone.

The journey to action begins in acceptance. God accepts you as you are. You don't have to clean up first before you meet God. You'll be relieved to discover that lots of other people—everyone, in fact—are as far from being cleaned up as you are. Acceptance means you can tell your story and receive God's grace for your circumstances, whatever they are. You're not alone. You can belong to a circle of friends that helps you move through what holds you back and find a place of hope.

Because of the safety of acceptance, you can venture into authenticity. Real life can be hard, but God is really there with you. Nothing can separate you from the love of God. *Nothing.* A moment can change your life if you embrace it as real. A moment of insight. A moment of calling. A moment of healing. You have a sure foundation that does not move. God's faithfulness is your hope. When you risk being real, you invite others into your life, and they help you learn that Jesus cares, whatever is going on in your life. What relationships are you missing out on because you hesitate to be real? Let others help you strip off the grave clothes and discover the new life God gives you.

When you experience authenticity, the world of affirmation opens. Your gifts flow from the character God is forming in you, and with your gifts you bless other people. You don't have to be perfect or a spiritual giant to find significance. Your circle of friends can affirm your gifts and healthy, timely ways to use them. Opportunities to put your gifts to work may be closer than you realize. Are you looking for the moments? Your gifts may be an expression of ministry, but they may also open doors to further ministry.

Acceptance, authenticity, and affirmation lay the groundwork for true accountability. In relationships of mutual accountability, you can receive the comfort of companionship on your journey. Others who know you well walk with you and help you keep your eye on the joy God has in store for you. They help you move through the hard places by being truthful with you, and you come out stronger on the other side. Rather than focusing on judgment, true accountability helps you choose to avoid the pitfalls that await you and keeps you squarely on the path God lays out. In relationships of accountability, you and your friends help each other sit at the feet of Jesus. You can't stay stuck in your past—your sin, your shame, your guilt, your regrets—and truly know the freedom Christ died to bring you.

Out of all this—acceptance, authenticity, affirmation, and accountability—flows action. God has a purpose for you. You'll have to risk not being 100 percent sure what will happen when you obey God's call. You have the opportunity to make yourself available to God with a willing spirit and open eyes to respond to the opportunities he's preparing you for. Are you close enough to hear God's voice? Do you approach God with a heart of worship and obedience? How is God calling you into the purpose he has for you? Perhaps God is calling you into a new way of experiencing him in worship and ministry. Perhaps he is calling you into a community outreach ministry. Perhaps he is calling you into leading other women in forming a circle of friends who multiply God's grace and mercy through genuine relationships.

It's time for action. What are you waiting for?

## FIND YOUR EXAMPLE IN THE BIBLE.

Does shame hold you back? Remember the Samaritan woman at the well who forgot her shame when she met Jesus, the Living Water.

Does fear hold you back? Remember the lesson from Mary Magdalene on the day of the resurrection. Fear is not the last word.

Do you feel exposed and naked? Remember the woman in John 8 who met Jesus the defender.

Do you feel overwhelmed by the demands of life? Think of the woman in Proverbs 31 who rested in God's character.

Do you feel let down by the way your life has turned out so far? Remember Tamar who clung to God's promise and did everything she could to receive his blessing.

Do you think you're too far away from the action to do any good? Consider Jael, whose opportunity to rescue a nation came right to her door.

Do you feel you don't know enough for effective ministry? Follow the example of Mary, who sat at Jesus' feet, and immerse yourself in God's Word.

Do you think you've made too many mistakes? Remember Bathsheba, who moved past regret and sorrow and found forgiveness and restoration.

Are you hesitant to take a risk? Remember Rahab, who saw an opportunity, took a risk, and trusted God for the outcome.

We get comfortable telling ourselves things that are not true—or at least not the whole story. We get comfortable with relationships that demand little of us. We get comfortable letting life happen to us, rather than stepping out with intention and courage. We convince ourselves that life is overwhelming without adding anything else. We persuade ourselves that we're not lonely or in pain. We believe that life will be better if we're careful not to disturb the delicate balance we've achieved.

But it doesn't have to be that way. Life can be full. Life can be rich. Life can mean something. Life can have purpose. And most of all, you are not alone. God is present in every circumstance, and he gives us people in our lives who can be a circle of friends to weep when we weep, to rejoice when we rejoice, to tell us the truth we're afraid to hear, to walk alongside us when we don't know the way.

It's time to step out of your comfort zone and into God's adventure. You can come as you are, and the adventure ahead of you is worth the risk of letting go of the familiar. No one else is you, so no one else can enrich others just the way you do. Freedom from what holds you back is a true option! Step into your journey. Walk in your purpose.

# LIVE TO PRAISE

Walking in a shadowland of broken dreams and shifting sand,
'Cause I gave my heart away too many times.
I didn't plan to meet You, meet there.
Your kindness took me by surprise.
As grace and mercy showered over me.

Now I live to praise, I live to praise You.
The Father's heart is full of love for me.
I live to praise, I live to praise You.
The lover of my soul has set me free.

You didn't tell me pretty lies, You told me all I tried to hide.
You knew the truth that I could not deny.
Pure love flowing down like rain.
A worship dance that lasts all day.
I couldn't help but fall in love with You.

Now I live to praise, I live to praise You.
I worship You, oh God, my worthy King.
I live to praise, I live to praise You.
You are my strength, my song, my everything.

Oh, Jesus, I fell in love with You, I finally found the truth.
Oh, Lord Jesus, now I live to bless Your name.
Now I live to bless Your name.

To hear Your voice, to feel you breathe,
I'm caught up in Your love for me.
A heavenly embrace that covers me.

I am humbled and amazed as I walk along the way.
As I walk along the way You planned for me.
Now I live to praise, I live to praise You.
The Father's heart is full of love for me.
I live to praise, I live to praise You.
The lover of my soul has set me free.
I live to praise, I live to praise You.

I worship You, O God, my worthy King.
I live to praise, I live to praise You.
You are my strength, my song, my everything.

—Lisa Troyer/Dawn Yoder
© 2010, McKinney Music/BMI (administered by
LifeWay Christian Resources)

# Reflections

🎵 How do the words of this song connect to your life?

🎵 How would you finish the sentence, "I need to trust God, but _____"? What holds you back?

🎵 What gets in the way of making yourself available and obedient to God's nudgings?

🎵 Consider what's closest to your heart and how you might turn that concern into a ministry opportunity.

🎵 Name four friends you could invite to join you in the adventure of Five Friends, Five Weeks.

# I FOUND GRACE

There were places in my heart
That I had never been to,
Roads I'd never traveled,
Trails I'd never walked.
There were mountains in the distance,
Valleys deep and wide,
Oceans just beyond my reach
And rivers cracked and dried.

It was hard to find my way
Through life's crazy, winding maze.

Then I found grace, I found love,
And a circle of friends who helped me find out who I was.
I found grace, I found a home,
A place to believe and become, and a place to belong.

There were places I was broken,
I didn't even know.
But I could hear their whispers
Haunt me like a ghost.
I didn't like what I was feeling.
I was scared to be alone.
'Cause those lost and frozen memories
Were chilling to the bone.

Then I found grace, I found love,
And a circle of friends who helped me find out who I was.
I found grace, I found a home.
A place to believe and become, and a place to belong.

—Dawn Yoder/Lisa Troyer/Paul Marino
© 2010, McKinney Music/BMI Van Ness Press/ASCAP
(administered by LifeWay Christian Resources)

You are important to God, and he wants to share his story of faith, hope, and love through you. You've read my story and the stories of other women who have been touched by Circle of Friends Ministries. My heart's desire is that you will find your place to belong, and that you will offer a place to belong to another woman searching for acceptance, authenticity, affirmation—and in time, accountability. Perhaps because of what God will do through you, she, too, will take action and walk in her God-given purpose.

I can't wait to hear your story. Visit our website at www.ourcircleoffriends.org and let us know how God is moving in your life and community. Listen to a radio broadcast or worship with us by downloading a free song. Learn more about how you can contribute to the Circle of Friends blog or devotionals

I pray that you will know God's grace in your life as you pursue your personal relationship with Jesus Christ. My hope is that you will share what God reveals to you and live it out in a circle of friends.

May God lead you to the place you belong.

—Lisa Troyer

# RESOURCES FOR
# YOUR CIRCLE OF FRIENDS

# ONE–YEAR BIBLE READING SCHEDULE

| | | | |
|---|---|---|---|
| 1–Jan | Gen. 1–2 | Matt. 1 | Ps. 1 |
| 2–Jan | Gen. 3–4 | Matt. 2 | Ps. 2 |
| 3–Jan | Gen. 5–7 | Matt. 3 | Ps. 3 |
| 4–Jan | Gen. 8–10 | Matt. 4 | Ps. 4 |
| 5–Jan | Gen. 11–13 | Matt. 5:1–20 | Ps. 5 |
| 6–Jan | Gen. 14–16 | Matt. 5:21–48 | Ps. 6 |
| 7–Jan | Gen. 17–18 | Matt. 6:1–18 | Ps. 7 |
| 8–Jan | Gen. 19–20 | Matt. 6:19–34 | Ps. 8 |
| 9–Jan | Gen. 21–23 | Matt. 7:1–11 | Ps. 9:1–8 |
| 10–Jan | Gen. 24 | Matt. 7:12–29 | Ps. 9:9–20 |
| 11–Jan | Gen. 25–26 | Matt. 8:1–17 | Ps. 10:1–11 |
| 12–Jan | Gen. 27:1–28:9 | Matt. 8:18–34 | Ps. 10:12–18 |
| 13–Jan | Gen. 28:10–29:35 | Matt. 9 | Ps. 11 |
| 14–Jan | Gen. 30:1–31:21 | Matt. 10:1–15 | Ps. 12 |
| 15–Jan | Gen. 31:22–32:21 | Matt. 10:16–36 | Ps. 13 |
| 16–Jan | Gen. 32:22–34:31 | Matt. 10:37–11:6 | Ps. 14 |
| 17–Jan | Gen. 35–36 | Matt. 11:7–24 | Ps. 15 |
| 18–Jan | Gen. 37–38 | Matt. 11:25–30 | Ps. 16 |
| 19–Jan | Gen. 39–40 | Matt. 12:1–29 | Ps. 17 |
| 20–Jan | Gen. 41 | Matt. 12:30–50 | Ps. 18:1–15 |
| 21–Jan | Gen. 42–43 | Matt. 13:1–9 | Ps. 18:16–29 |
| 22–Jan | Gen. 44–45 | Matt. 13:10–23 | Ps. 18:30–50 |
| 23–Jan | Gen. 46:1–47:26 | Matt. 13:24–43 | Ps. 19 |
| 24–Jan | Gen. 47:27–49:28 | Matt. 13:44–58 | Ps. 20 |
| 25–Jan | Gen. 49:29–Exod. 1:22 | Matt. 14 | Ps. 21 |
| 26–Jan | Exod. 2–3 | Matt. 15:1–28 | Ps. 22:1–21 |
| 27–Jan | Exod. 4:1–5:21 | Matt. 15:29–16:12 | Ps. 22:22–31 |
| 28–Jan | Exod. 5:22–7:24 | Matt. 16:13–28 | Ps. 23 |
| 29–Jan | Exod. 7:25–9:35 | Matt. 17:1–9 | Ps. 24 |
| 30–Jan | Exod. 10–11 | Matt. 17:10–27 | Ps. 25 |
| 31–Jan | Exod. 12 | Matt. 18:1–20 | Ps. 26 |
| 1–Feb | Exod. 13–14 | Matt. 18:21–35 | Ps. 27 |
| 2–Feb | Exod. 15–16 | Matt. 19:1–15 | Ps. 28 |
| 3–Feb | Exod. 17–19 | Matt. 19:16–30 | Ps. 29 |
| 4–Feb | Exod. 20–21 | Matt. 20:1–19 | Ps. 30 |
| 5–Feb | Exod. 22–23 | Matt. 20:20–34 | Ps. 31:1–8 |
| 6–Feb | Exod. 24–25 | Matt. 21:1–27 | Ps. 31:9–18 |
| 7–Feb | Exod 26–27 | Matt. 21:28–46 | Ps. 31:19–24 |
| 8–Feb | Exod. 28 | Matt. 22 | Ps. 32 |
| 9–Feb | Exod. 29 | Matt. 23:1–36 | Ps. 33:1–12 |
| 10–Feb | Exod. 30–31 | Matt. 23:37–24:28 | Ps. 33:13–22 |
| 11–Feb | Exod. 32–33 | Matt. 24:29–51 | Ps. 34:1–7 |
| 12–Feb | Exod. 34:1–35:29 | Matt. 25:1–13 | Ps. 34:8–22 |
| 13–Feb | Exod. 35:30–37:29 | Matt. 25:14–30 | Ps. 35:1–8 |
| 14–Feb | Exod. 38–39 | Matt. 25:31–46 | Ps. 35:9–17 |

| | | | |
|---|---|---|---|
| 15–Feb | Exod. 40 | Matt. 26:1–35 | Ps. 35:18–28 |
| 16–Feb | Lev. 1–3 | Matt. 26:36–68 | Ps. 36:1–6 |
| 17–Feb | Lev. 4:1–5:13 | Matt. 26:69–27:26 | Ps. 36:7–12 |
| 18–Feb | Lev. 5:14 –7:21 | Matt. 27:27–50 | Ps. 37:1–6 |
| 19–Feb | Lev. 7:22–8:36 | Matt. 27:51–66 | Ps. 37:7–26 |
| 20–Feb | Lev. 9–10 | Matt. 28 | Ps. 37:27–40 |
| 21–Feb | Lev. 11–12 | Mark 1:1–28 | Ps. 38 |
| 22–Feb | Lev. 13 | Mark 1:29–39 | Ps. 39 |
| 23–Feb | Lev. 14 | Mark 1:40–2:12 | Ps. 40:1–8 |
| 24–Feb | Lev. 15 | Mark 2:13–3:35 | Ps. 40:9–17 |
| 25–Feb | Lev. 16–17 | Mark 4:1–20 | Ps. 41:1–4 |
| 26–Feb | Lev. 18–19 | Mark 4:21–41 | Ps. 41:5–13 |
| 27–Feb | Lev. 20 | Mark 5 | Ps. 42–43 |
| 28–Feb | Lev. 21–22 | Mark 6:1–13 | Ps. 44 |
| 1–Mar | Lev. 23–24 | Mark 6:14–29 | Ps. 45:1–5 |
| 2–Mar | Lev. 25 | Mark 6:30–56 | Ps. 45:6–12 |
| 3–Mar | Lev. 26 | Mark 7 | Ps. 45:13–17 |
| 4–Mar | Lev. 27 | Mark 8 | Ps. 46 |
| 5–Mar | Num. 1–2 | Mark 9:1–13 | Ps. 47 |
| 6–Mar | Num. 3 | Mark 9:14–50 | Ps. 48:1–8 |
| 7–Mar | Num. 4 | Mark 10:1–34 | Ps. 48:9–14 |
| 8–Mar | Num. 5:1–6:21 | Mark 10:35–52 | Ps. 49:1–9 |
| 9–Mar | Num. 6:22–7:47 | Mark 11 | Ps. 49:10–20 |
| 10–Mar | Num. 7:48–8:4 | Mark 12:1–27 | Ps. 50:1–15 |
| 11–Mar | Num. 8:5–9:23 | Mark 12:28–44 | Ps. 50:16–23 |
| 12–Mar | Num. 10–11 | Mark 13:1–8 | Ps. 51:1–9 |
| 13–Mar | Num. 12–13 | Mark 13:9–37 | Ps. 51:10–19 |
| 14–Mar | Num. 14 | Mark 14:1–31 | Ps. 52 |
| 15–Mar | Num. 15 | Mark 14:32–72 | Ps. 53 |
| 16–Mar | Num. 16 | Mark 15:1–32 | Ps. 54 |
| 17–Mar | Num. 17–18 | Mark 15:33–47 | Ps. 55 |
| 18–Mar | Num. 19–20 | Mark 16 | Ps. 56:1–7 |
| 19–Mar | Num. 21:1–22:20 | Luke 1:1–25 | Ps. 56:8–13 |
| 20–Mar | Num. 22:21–23:30 | Luke 1:26–56 | Ps. 57 |
| 21–Mar | Num. 24–25 | Luke 1:57–2:20 | Ps. 58 |
| 22–Mar | Num. 26:1–27:11 | Luke 2:21–38 | Ps. 59:1–8 |
| 23–Mar | Num. 27:12–29:11 | Luke 2:39–52 | Ps. 59:9–17 |
| 24–Mar | Num. 29:12–30:16 | Luke 3 | Ps. 60:1–5 |
| 25–Mar | Num. 31 | Luke 4 | Ps. 60:6–12 |
| 26–Mar | Num. 32–33 | Luke 5:1–16 | Ps. 61 |
| 27–Mar | Num. 34–36 | Luke 5:17–32 | Ps. 62:1–6 |
| 28–Mar | Deut. 1:1–2:25 | Luke 5:33–6:11 | Ps. 62:7–12 |
| 29–Mar | Deut. 2:26–4:14 | Luke 6:12–35 | Ps. 63:1–5 |
| 30–Mar | Deut. 4:15–5:22 | Luke 6:36–49 | Ps. 63:6–11 |
| 31–Mar | Deut. 5:23–7:26 | Luke 7:1–17 | Ps. 64:1–5 |
| 1–Apr | Deut. 8–9 | Luke 7:18–35 | Ps. 64:6–10 |
| 2–Apr | Deut. 10–11 | Luke 7:36–8:3 | Ps. 65:1–8 |

| | | | |
|---|---|---|---|
| 3–Apr | Deut. 12–13 | Luke 8:4–21 | Ps. 65:9–13 |
| 4–Apr | Deut. 14:1–16:8 | Luke 8:22–39 | Ps. 66:1–7 |
| 5–Apr | Deut. 16:9–18:22 | Luke 8:40–56 | Ps. 66:8–15 |
| 6–Apr | Deut. 19:1–21:9 | Luke 9:1–22 | Ps. 66:16–20 |
| 7–Apr | Deut. 21:10–23:8 | Luke 9:23–42 | Ps. 67 |
| 8–Apr | Deut. 23:9–25:19 | Luke 9:43–62 | Ps. 68:1–6 |
| 9–Apr | Deut. 26:1–28:14 | Luke 10:1–20 | Ps. 68:7–14 |
| 10–Apr | Deut. 28:15–68 | Luke 10:21–37 | Ps. 68:15–19 |
| 11–Apr | Deut. 29–30 | Luke 10:38–11:23 | Ps. 68:20–27 |
| 12–Apr | Deut. 31:1–32:22 | Luke 11:24–36 | Ps. 68:28–35 |
| 13–Apr | Deut. 32:23–33:29 | Luke 11:37–54 | Ps. 69:1–9 |
| 14–Apr | Deut. 34–Josh. 2 | Luke 12:1–15 | Ps. 69:10–17 |
| 15–Apr | Josh. 3:1–5:12 | Luke 12:16–40 | Ps. 69:18–28 |
| 16–Apr | Josh. 5:13–7:26 | Luke 12:41–48 | Ps. 69:29–36 |
| 17–Apr | Josh. 8–9 | Luke 12:49–59 | Ps. 70 |
| 18–Apr | Josh. 10:1–11:15 | Luke 13:1–21 | Ps. 71:1–6 |
| 19–Apr | Josh. 11:16–13:33 | Luke 13:22–35 | Ps. 71:7–16 |
| 20–Apr | Josh. 14–16 | Luke 14:1–15 | Ps. 71:17–21 |
| 21–Apr | Josh. 17:1–19:16 | Luke 14:16–35 | Ps. 71:22–24 |
| 22–Apr | Josh. 19:17–21:42 | Luke 15:1–10 | Ps. 72:1–11 |
| 23–Apr | Josh. 21:43–22:34 | Luke 15:11–32 | Ps. 72:12–20 |
| 24–Apr | Josh. 23–24 | Luke 16:1–18 | Ps. 73:1–9 |
| 25–Apr | Judg. 1–2 | Luke 16:19–17:10 | Ps. 73:10–20 |
| 26–Apr | Judg. 3–4 | Luke 17:11–37 | Ps. 73:21–28 |
| 27–Apr | Judg. 5:1–6:24 | Luke 18:1–17 | Ps. 74:1–3 |
| 28–Apr | Judg. 6:25–7:25 | Luke 18:18–43 | Ps. 74:4–11 |
| 29–Apr | Judg. 8:1–9:23 | Luke 19:1–28 | Ps. 74:12–17 |
| 30–Apr | Judg. 9:24–10:18 | Luke 19:29–48 | Ps. 74:18–23 |
| 1–May | Judg. 11:1–12:7 | Luke 20:1–26 | Ps. 75:1–7 |
| 2–May | Judg. 12:8–14:20 | Luke 20:27–47 | Ps. 75:8–10 |
| 3–May | Judg. 15–16 | Luke 21:1–19 | Ps. 76:1–7 |
| 4–May | Judg. 17–18 | Luke 21:20–22:6 | Ps. 76:8–12 |
| 5–May | Judg. 19:1–20:23 | Luke 22:7–30 | Ps. 77:1–11 |
| 6–May | Judg. 20:24–21:25 | Luke 22:31–54 | Ps. 77:12–20 |
| 7–May | Ruth 1–2 | Luke 22:55–23:25 | Ps. 78:1–4 |
| 8–May | Ruth 3–4 | Luke 23:26–24:12 | Ps. 78:5–8 |
| 9–May | 1 Sam. 1:1–2:21 | Luke 24:13–53 | Ps. 78:9–16 |
| 10–May | 1 Sam. 2:22–4:22 | John 1:1–28 | Ps. 78:17–24 |
| 11–May | 1 Sam. 5–7 | John 1:29–51 | Ps. 78:25–33 |
| 12–May | 1 Sam. 8:1–9:26 | John 2 | Ps. 78:34–41 |
| 13–May | 1 Sam. 9:27–11:15 | John 3:1–22 | Ps. 78:42–55 |
| 14–May | 1 Sam. 12–13 | John 3:23–4:10 | Ps. 78:56–66 |
| 15–May | 1 Sam. 14 | John 4:11–38 | Ps. 78:67–72 |
| 16–May | 1 Sam. 15–16 | John 4:39–54 | Ps. 79:1–7 |
| 17–May | 1 Sam. 17 | John 5:1–24 | Ps. 79:8–13 |
| 18–May | 1 Sam. 18–19 | John 5:25–47 | Ps. 80:1–7 |
| 19–May | 1 Sam. 20–21 | John 6:1–21 | Ps. 80:8–19 |

| | | | |
|---|---|---|---|
| 20–May | 1 Sam. 22–23 | John 6:22–42 | Ps. 81:1–10 |
| 21–May | 1 Sam. 24:1–25:31 | John 6:43–71 | Ps. 81:11–16 |
| 22–May | 1 Sam. 25:32–27:12 | John 7:1–24 | Ps. 82 |
| 23–May | 1 Sam. 28–29 | John 7:25–8:11 | Ps. 83 |
| 24–May | 1 Sam. 30–31 | John 8:12–47 | Ps. 84:1–4 |
| 25–May | 2 Sam. 1–2 | John 8:48–9:12 | Ps. 84:5–12 |
| 26–May | 2 Sam. 3–4 | John 9:13–34 | Ps. 85:1–7 |
| 27–May | 2 Sam. 5:1–7:17 | John 9:35–10:10 | Ps. 85:8–13 |
| 28–May | 2 Sam. 7:18–10:19 | John 10:11–30 | Ps. 86:1–10 |
| 29–May | 2 Sam. 11:1–12:25 | John 10:31–11:16 | Ps. 86:11–17 |
| 30–May | 2 Sam. 12:26–13:39 | John 11:17–54 | Ps. 87 |
| 31–May | 2 Sam. 14:1–15:12 | John 11:55–12:19 | Ps. 88:1–9 |
| 1–Jun | 2 Sam. 15:13–16:23 | John 12:20–43 | Ps. 88:10–18 |
| 2–Jun | 2 Sam. 17:1–18:18 | John 12:44–13:20 | Ps. 89:1–6 |
| 3–Jun | 2 Sam. 18:19–19:39 | John 13:21–38 | Ps. 89:7–13 |
| 4–Jun | 2 Sam. 19:40–21:22 | John 14:1–17 | Ps. 89:14–18 |
| 5–Jun | 2 Sam. 22:1–23:7 | John 14:18–15:27 | Ps. 89:19–29 |
| 6–Jun | 2 Sam. 23:8–24:25 | John 16:1–22 | Ps. 89:30–37 |
| 7–Jun | 1 Kings 1 | John 16:23–17:5 | Ps. 89:38–52 |
| 8–Jun | 1 Kings 2 | John 17:6–26 | Ps. 90:1–12 |
| 9–Jun | 1 Kings 3–4 | John 18:1–27 | Ps. 90:13–17 |
| 10–Jun | 1 Kings 5–6 | John 18:28–19:5 | Ps. 91:1–10 |
| 11–Jun | 1 Kings 7 | John 19:6–25a | Ps. 91:11–16 |
| 12–Jun | 1 Kings 8:1–53 | John 19:25b–42 | Ps. 92:1–9 |
| 13–Jun | 1 Kings 8:54–10:13 | John 20:1–18 | Ps. 92:10–15 |
| 14–Jun | 1 Kings 10:14–11:43 | John 20:19–31 | Ps. 93 |
| 15–Jun | 1 Kings 12:1–13:10 | John 21 | Ps. 94:1–11 |
| 16–Jun | 1 Kings 13:11–14:31 | Acts 1:1–11 | Ps. 94:12–23 |
| 17–Jun | 1 Kings 15:1–16:20 | Acts 1:12–26 | Ps. 95 |
| 18–Jun | 1 Kings 16:21–18:19 | Acts 2:1–21 | Ps. 96:1–8 |
| 19–Jun | 1 Kings 18:20–19:21 | Acts 2:22–41 | Ps. 96:9–13 |
| 20–Jun | 1 Kings 20 | Acts 2:42–3:26 | Ps. 97:1–6 |
| 21–Jun | 1 Kings 21:1–22:28 | Acts 4:1–22 | Ps. 97:7–12 |
| 22–Jun | 1 Kings 22:29–2 Kings 1:18 | Acts 4:23–5:11 | Ps. 98 |
| 23–Jun | 2 Kings 2–3 | Acts 5:12–28 | Ps. 99 |
| 24–Jun | 2 Kings 4 | Acts 5:29–6:15 | Ps. 100 |
| 25–Jun | 2 Kings 5:1–6:23 | Acts 7:1–16 | Ps. 101 |
| 26–Jun | 2 Kings 6:24–8:15 | Acts 7:17–36 | Ps. 102:1–7 |
| 27–Jun | 2 Kings 8:16–9:37 | Acts 7:37–53 | Ps. 102:8–17 |
| 28–Jun | 2 Kings 10–11 | Acts 7:54–8:8 | Ps. 102:18–28 |
| 29–Jun | 2 Kings 12–13 | Acts 8:9–40 | Ps. 103:1–9 |
| 30–Jun | 2 Kings 14–15 | Acts 9:1–16 | Ps. 103:10–14 |
| 1–Jul | 2 Kings 16–17 | Acts 9:17–31 | Ps. 103:15–22 |
| 2–Jul | 2 Kings 18:1–19:7 | Acts 9:32–10:16 | Ps. 104:1–9 |
| 3–Jul | 2 Kings 19:8–20:21 | Acts 10:17–33 | Ps. 104:10–23 |
| 4–Jul | 2 Kings 21:1–22:20 | Acts 10:34–11:18 | Ps. 104: 24–30 |
| 5–Jul | 2 Kings 23 | Acts 11:19–12:17 | Ps. 104:31–35 |

| | | | |
|---|---|---|---|
| 6–Jul | 2 Kings 24–25 | Acts 12:18–13:13 | Ps. 105:1–7 |
| 7–Jul | 1 Chron. 1–2 | Acts 13:14–43 | Ps. 105:8–15 |
| 8–Jul | 1 Chron. 3:1–5:10 | Acts 13:44–14:10 | Ps. 105:16–28 |
| 9–Jul | 1 Chron. 5:11–6:81 | Acts 14:11–28 | Ps. 105:29–36 |
| 10–Jul | 1 Chron. 7:1–9:9 | Acts 15:1–18 | Ps. 105:37–45 |
| 11–Jul | 1 Chron. 9:10–11:9 | Acts 15:19–41 | Ps. 106:1–12 |
| 12–Jul | 1 Chron. 11:10–12:40 | Acts 16:1–15 | Ps. 106:13–27 |
| 13–Jul | 1 Chron. 13–15 | Acts 16:16–40 | Ps. 106:28–33 |
| 14–Jul | 1 Chron. 16–17 | Acts 17:1–14 | Ps. 106:34–43 |
| 15–Jul | 1 Chron. 18–20 | Acts 17:15–34 | Ps. 106:44–48 |
| 16–Jul | 1 Chron. 21–22 | Acts 18:1–23 | Ps. 107:1–9 |
| 17–Jul | 1 Chron. 23–25 | Acts 18:24–19:10 | Ps. 107:10–16 |
| 18–Jul | 1 Chron. 26–27 | Acts 19:11–22 | Ps. 107:17–32 |
| 19–Jul | 1 Chron. 28–29 | Acts 19:23–41 | Ps. 107:33–38 |
| 20–Jul | 2 Chron. 1–3 | Acts 20:1–16 | Ps. 107:39–43 |
| 21–Jul | 2 Chron. 4:1–6:11 | Acts 20:17–38 | Ps. 108 |
| 22–Jul | 2 Chron. 6:12–7:10 | Acts 21:1–14 | Ps. 109:1–20 |
| 23–Jul | 2 Chron. 7:11–9:28 | Acts 21:15–32 | Ps. 109:21–31 |
| 24–Jul | 2 Chron. 9:29–12:16 | Acts 21:33–22:16 | Ps. 110:1–3 |
| 25–Jul | 2 Chron. 13–15 | Acts 22:17–23:11 | Ps. 110:4–7 |
| 26–Jul | 2 Chron. 16–17 | Acts 23:12–24:21 | Ps. 111 |
| 27–Jul | 2 Chron. 18–19 | Acts 24:22–25:12 | Ps. 112 |
| 28–Jul | 2 Chron. 20–21 | Acts 25:13–27 | Ps. 113 |
| 29–Jul | 2 Chron. 22–23 | Acts 26 | Ps. 114 |
| 30–Jul | 2 Chron. 24:1–25:16 | Acts 27:1–20 | Ps. 115:1–10 |
| 31–Jul | 2 Chron. 25:17–27:9 | Acts 27:21–28:6 | Ps. 115:11–18 |
| 1–Aug | 2 Chron. 28:1–29:19 | Acts 28:7–31 | Ps. 116:1–5 |
| 2–Aug | 2 Chron. 29:20–30:27 | Rom. 1:1–17 | Ps. 116:6–19 |
| 3–Aug | 2 Chron. 31–32 | Rom. 1:18–32 | Ps. 117 |
| 4–Aug | 2 Chron. 33:1–34:7 | Rom. 2 | Ps. 118:1–18 |
| 5–Aug | 2 Chron. 34:8–35:19 | Rom. 3:1–26 | Ps. 118:19–23 |
| 6–Aug | 2 Chron. 35:20–36:23 | Rom. 3:27–4:25 | Ps. 118:24–29 |
| 7–Aug | Ezra 1–3 | Rom. 5 | Ps. 119:1–8 |
| 8–Aug | Ezra 4–5 | Rom. 6:1–7:6 | Ps. 119:9–16 |
| 9–Aug | Ezra 6:1–7:26 | Rom. 7:7–25 | Ps. 119:17–32 |
| 10–Aug | Ezra 7:27–9:4 | Rom. 8:1–27 | Ps. 119:33–40 |
| 11–Aug | Ezra 9:5–10:44 | Rom. 8:28–39 | Ps. 119:41–64 |
| 12–Aug | Neh. 1:1–3:16 | Rom. 9:1–18 | Ps. 119:65–72 |
| 13–Aug | Neh. 3:17–5:13 | Rom. 9:19–33 | Ps. 119:73–80 |
| 14–Aug | Neh. 5:14–7:73 | Rom. 10:1–13 | Ps. 119:81–88 |
| 15–Aug | Neh. 8:1–9:5 | Rom. 10:14–11:24 | Ps. 119:89–104 |
| 16–Aug | Neh. 9:6–10:27 | Rom. 11:25–12:8 | Ps. 119:105–120 |
| 17–Aug | Neh. 10:28–12:26 | Rom. 12:9–13:7 | Ps. 119:121–128 |
| 18–Aug | Neh. 12:27–13:31 | Rom. 13:8–14:12 | Ps. 119:129–136 |
| 19–Aug | Esther 1:1–2:18 | Rom. 14:13–15:13 | Ps. 119:137–152 |
| 20–Aug | Esther 2:19–5:14 | Rom. 15:14–21 | Ps. 119:153–168 |
| 21–Aug | Esther. 6–8 | Rom. 15:22–33 | Ps. 119:169–176 |

| | | | |
|---|---|---|---|
| 22–Aug | Esther 9–10 | Rom. 16 | Ps. 120–122 |
| 23–Aug | Job 1–3 | 1 Cor. 1:1–25 | Ps. 123 |
| 24–Aug | Job 4–6 | 1 Cor. 1:26–2:16 | Ps. 124–125 |
| 25–Aug | Job 7–9 | 1 Cor. 3 | Ps. 126–127 |
| 26–Aug | Job 10–13 | 1 Cor. 4:1–13 | Ps. 128–129 |
| 27–Aug | Job 14–16 | 1 Cor. 4:14–5:13 | Ps. 130 |
| 28–Aug | Job 17–20 | 1 Cor. 6 | Ps. 131 |
| 29–Aug | Job 21–23 | 1 Cor. 7:1–16 | Ps. 132 |
| 30–Aug | Job 24–27 | 1 Cor. 7:17–40 | Ps. 133–134 |
| 31–Aug | Job 28–30 | 1 Cor. 8 | Ps. 135 |
| 1–Sep | Job 31–33 | 1 Cor. 9:1–18 | Ps. 136:1–9 |
| 2–Sep | Job 34–36 | 1 Cor. 9:19–10:13 | Ps. 136:10–26 |
| 3–Sep | Job 37–39 | 1 Cor. 10:14–11:1 | Ps. 137 |
| 4–Sep | Job 40–42 | 1 Cor. 11:2–34 | Ps. 138 |
| 5–Sep | Eccles. 1:1–3:15 | 1 Cor. 12:1–26 | Ps. 139:1–6 |
| 6–Sep | Eccles. 3:16–6:12 | 1 Cor. 12:27–13:13 | Ps. 139:7–18 |
| 7–Sep | Eccles. 7:1–9:12 | 1 Cor. 14:1–22 | Ps. 139:19–24 |
| 8–Sep | Eccles. 9:13–12:14 | 1 Cor. 14:23–15:11 | Ps. 140:1–8 |
| 9–Sep | SS 1–4 | 1 Cor. 15:12–34 | Ps. 140:9–13 |
| 10–Sep | SS 5–8 | 1 Cor. 15:35–58 | Ps. 141 |
| 11–Sep | Isa. 1–2 | 1 Cor. 16 | Ps. 142 |
| 12–Sep | Isa. 3–5 | 2 Cor. 1:1–11 | Ps. 143:1–6 |
| 13–Sep | Isa. 6–8 | 2 Cor. 1:12–2:4 | Ps. 143:7–12 |
| 14–Sep | Isa. 9–10 | 2 Cor. 2:5–17 | Ps. 144 |
| 15–Sep | Isa. 11–13 | 2 Cor. 3 | Ps. 145 |
| 16–Sep | Isa. 14–16 | 2 Cor. 4 | Ps. 146 |
| 17–Sep | Isa. 17–19 | 2 Cor. 5 | Ps. 147:1–11 |
| 18–Sep | Isa. 20–23 | 2 Cor. 6 | Ps. 147:12–20 |
| 19–Sep | Isa. 24:1–26:19 | 2 Cor. 7 | Ps. 148 |
| 20–Sep | Isa. 26:20–28:29 | 2 Cor. 8 | Ps. 149–150 |
| 21–Sep | Isa. 29–30 | 2 Cor. 9 | Prov. 1:1–9 |
| 22–Sep | Isa. 31–33 | 2 Cor. 10 | Prov. 1:10–22 |
| 23–Sep | Isa. 34–36 | 2 Cor. 11 | Prov. 1:23–26 |
| 24–Sep | Isa. 37–38 | 2 Cor. 12:1–10 | Prov. 1:27–33 |
| 25–Sep | Isa. 39–40 | 2 Cor. 12:11–13:14 | Prov. 2:1–15 |
| 26–Sep | Isa. 41–42 | Gal. 1 | Prov. 2:16–22 |
| 27–Sep | Isa. 43:1–44:20 | Gal. 2 | Prov. 3:1–12 |
| 28–Sep | Isa. 44:21–46:13 | Gal. 3:1–18 | Prov. 3:13–26 |
| 29–Sep | Isa. 47:1–49:13 | Gal 3:19–29 | Prov. 3:27–35 |
| 30–Sep | Isa. 49:14–51:23 | Gal 4:1–11 | Prov. 4:1–19 |
| 1–Oct | Isa. 52–54 | Gal. 4:12–31 | Prov. 4:20–27 |
| 2–Oct | Isa. 55–57 | Gal. 5 | Prov. 5:1–14 |
| 3–Oct | Isa. 58–59 | Gal. 6 | Prov. 5:15–23 |
| 4–Oct | Isa. 60–62 | Eph. 1 | Prov. 6:1–5 |
| 5–Oct | Isa. 63:1–65:16 | Eph. 2 | Prov. 6:6–19 |
| 6–Oct | Isa. 65:17–66:24 | Eph. 3:1–4:16 | Prov. 6:20–26 |

| | | | |
|---|---|---|---|
| 7–Oct | Jer. 1–2 | Eph. 4:17–32 | Prov. 6:27–35 |
| 8–Oct | Jer. 3:1–4:22 | Eph. 5 | Prov. 7:1–5 |
| 9–Oct | Jer. 4:23–5:31 | Eph. 6 | Prov. 7:6–27 |
| 10–Oct | Jer. 6:1–7:26 | Phil. 1:1–26 | Prov. 8:1–11 |
| 11–Oct | Jer. 7:26–9:16 | Phil. 1:27–2:18 | Prov. 8:12–21 |
| 12–Oct | Jer. 9:17–11:17 | Phil 2:19–30 | Prov. 8:22–36 |
| 13–Oct | Jer. 11:18–13:27 | Phil. 3 | Prov. 9:1–6 |
| 14–Oct | Jer. 14–15 | Phil. 4 | Prov. 9:7–18 |
| 15–Oct | Jer. 16–17 | Col. 1:1–23 | Prov. 10:1–5 |
| 16–Oct | Jer. 18:1–20:6 | Col. 1:24–2:15 | Prov. 10:6–14 |
| 17–Oct | Jer. 20:7–22:19 | Col. 2:16–3:4 | Prov. 10:15–26 |
| 18–Oct | Jer. 22:20–23:40 | Col. 3:5–4:1 | Prov. 10:27–32 |
| 19–Oct | Jer. 24–25 | Col. 4:2–18 | Prov. 11:1–11 |
| 20–Oct | Jer. 26–27 | 1 Thess. 1:1–2:8 | Prov. 11:12–21 |
| 21–Oct | Jer. 28–29 | 1 Thess. 2:9–3:13 | Prov. 11:22–26 |
| 22–Oct | Jer. 30:1–31:22 | 1 Thess. 4:1–5:11 | Prov. 11:27–31 |
| 23–Oct | Jer. 31:23–32:35 | 1 Thess. 5:12–28 | Prov. 12:1–14 |
| 24–Oct | Jer. 32:36–34:7 | 2 Thess. 1–2 | Prov. 12:15–20 |
| 25–Oct | Jer. 34:8–36:10 | 2 Thess. 3 | Prov. 12:21–28 |
| 26–Oct | Jer. 36:11–38:13 | 1 Tim. 1:1–17 | Prov. 13:1–4 |
| 27–Oct | Jer. 38:14–40:6 | 1 Tim. 1:18–3:13 | Prov. 13:5–13 |
| 28–Oct | Jer. 40:7–42:22 | 1 Tim. 3:14–4:10 | Prov. 13:14–21 |
| 29–Oct | Jer. 43–44 | 1 Tim. 4:11–5:16 | Prov. 13:22–25 |
| 30–Oct | Jer. 45–47 | 1 Tim. 5:17–6:21 | Prov. 14:1–6 |
| 31–Oct | Jer. 48:1–49:6 | 2 Tim. 1 | Prov. 14:7–22 |
| 1–Nov | Jer. 49:7–50:16 | 2 Tim. 2 | Prov. 14:23–27 |
| 2–Nov | Jer. 50:17–51:14 | 2 Tim. 3 | Prov. 14:28–35 |
| 3–Nov | Jer. 51:15–64 | 2 Tim. 4 | Prov. 15:1–9 |
| 4–Nov | Jer. 52–Lam. 1 | Titus 1:1–9 | Prov. 15:10–17 |
| 5–Nov | Lam. 2:1–3:38 | Titus 1:10–2:15 | Prov. 15:18–26 |
| 6–Nov | Lam. 3:39–5:22 | Titus 3 | Prov. 15:27–33 |
| 7–Nov | Ezek. 1:1–3:21 | Philemon 1 | Prov. 16:1–9 |
| 8–Nov | Ezek. 3:22–5:17 | Heb. 1:1–2:4 | Prov. 16:10–21 |
| 9–Nov | Ezek. 6–7 | Heb. 2:5–18 | Prov. 16:22–33 |
| 10–Nov | Ezek. 8–10 | Heb. 3:1–4:3 | Prov. 17:1–5 |
| 11–Nov | Ezek. 11–12 | Heb. 4:4–5:10 | Prov. 17:6–12 |
| 12–Nov | Ezek. 13–14 | Heb. 5:11–6:20 | Prov. 17:13–22 |
| 13–Nov | Ezek. 15:1–16:43 | Heb. 7:1–28 | Prov. 17:23–28 |
| 14–Nov | Ezek. 16:44–17:24 | Heb. 8:1–9:10 | Prov. 18:1–7 |
| 15–Nov | Ezek. 18–19 | Heb. 9:11–28 | Prov. 18:8–17 |
| 16–Nov | Ezek. 20 | Heb. 10:1–25 | Prov. 18:18–24 |
| 17–Nov | Ezek. 21–22 | Heb. 10:26–39 | Prov. 19:1–8 |
| 18–Nov | Ezek. 23 | Heb. 11:1–31 | Prov. 19:9–14 |
| 19–Nov | Ezek. 24–26 | Heb. 11:32–40 | Prov. 19:15–21 |
| 20–Nov | Ezek. 27–28 | Heb. 12:1–13 | Prov. 19:22–29 |
| 21–Nov | Ezek. 29–30 | Heb. 12:14–29 | Prov. 20:1–18 |

| | | | | |
|---|---|---|---|---|
| 22–Nov | Ezek. 31–32 | Heb. 13 | Prov. 20:19–24 |
| 23–Nov | Ezek. 33:1–34:10 | Jas. 1 | Prov. 20:25–30 |
| 24–Nov | Ezek. 34:11–36:15 | Jas. 2 | Prov. 21:1–8 |
| 25–Nov | Ezek. 36:16–37:28 | Jas. 3 | Prov. 21:9–18 |
| 26–Nov | Ezek. 38–39 | Jas. 4:1–5:6 | Prov. 21:19–24 |
| 27–Nov | Ezek. 40 | Jas. 5:7–20 | Prov. 21:25–31 |
| 28–Nov | Ezek. 41:1–43:12 | 1 Pet. 1:1–12 | Prov. 22:1–9 |
| 29–Nov | Ezek. 43:13–44:31 | 1 Pet. 1:13–2:3 | Prov. 22:10–23 |
| 30–Nov | Ezek. 45–46 | 1 Pet. 2:4–17 | Prov. 22:24–29 |
| 1–Dec | Ezek. 47–48 | 1 Pet. 2:18–3:7 | Prov. 23:1–9 |
| 2–Dec | Dan. 1:1–2:23 | 1 Pet. 3:8–4:19 | Prov. 23:10–16 |
| 3–Dec | Dan. 2:24–3:30 | 1 Pet. 5 | Prov. 23:17–25 |
| 4–Dec | Dan. 4 | 2 Pet. 1 | Prov. 23:26–35 |
| 5–Dec | Dan. 5 | 2 Pet. 2 | Prov. 24:1–18 |
| 6–Dec | Dan. 6:1–7:14 | 2 Pet. 3 | Prov. 24:19–27 |
| 7–Dec | Dan. 7:15–8:27 | 1 John 1:1–2:17 | Prov. 24:28–34 |
| 8–Dec | Dan. 9–10 | 1 John 2:18–29 | Prov. 25:1–12 |
| 9–Dec | Dan. 11–12 | 1 John 3:1–12 | Prov. 25:13–17 |
| 10–Dec | Hos. 1–3 | 1 John 3:13–4:16 | Prov. 25:18–28 |
| 11–Dec | Hos. 4–6 | 1 John 4:17–5:21 | Prov. 26:1–16 |
| 12–Dec | Hos. 7–10 | 2 John | Prov. 26:17–21 |
| 13–Dec | Hos. 11–14 | 3 John | Prov. 26:22–27:9 |
| 14–Dec | Joel 1:1–2:17 | Jude | Prov. 27:10–17 |
| 15–Dec | Joel 2:18–3:21 | Rev. 1:1–2:11 | Prov. 27:18–27 |
| 16–Dec | Amos 1:1–4:5 | Rev. 2:12–29 | Prov. 28:1–8 |
| 17–Dec | Amos 4:6–6:14 | Rev. 3 | Prov. 28:9–16 |
| 18–Dec | Amos 7–9 | Rev. 4:1–5:5 | Prov. 28:17–24 |
| 19–Dec | Obad.–Jonah | Rev. 5:6–14 | Prov. 28:25–28 |
| 20–Dec | Mic. 1:1–4:5 | Rev. 6:1–7:8 | Prov. 29:1–8 |
| 21–Dec | Mic. 4:6–7:20 | Rev. 7:9–8:13 | Prov. 29:9–14 |
| 22–Dec | Nah. 1–3 | Rev. 9–10 | Prov. 29:15–23 |
| 23–Dec | Hab. 1–3 | Rev. 11 | Prov. 29:24–27 |
| 24–Dec | Zeph. 1–3 | Rev. 12 | Prov. 30:1–6 |
| 25–Dec | Hag. 1–2 | Rev. 13:1–14:13 | Prov. 30:7–16 |
| 26–Dec | Zech. 1–4 | Rev. 14:14–16:3 | Prov. 30:17–20 |
| 27–Dec | Zech. 5–8 | Rev. 16:4–21 | Prov. 30:21–28 |
| 28–Dec | Zech. 9–11 | Rev. 17:1–18:8 | Prov. 30:29–33 |
| 29–Dec | Zech. 12–14 | Rev. 18:9–24 | Prov. 31:1–9 |
| 30–Dec | Mal. 1–2 | Rev. 19–20 | Prov. 31:10–17 |
| 31–Dec | Mal. 3–4 | Rev. 21–22 | Prov. 31:18–31 |

# Tips for Leading
# a Small Group

Whether you are an experienced small-group leader or venturing into new territory, here are a few tips to point you toward success.

**Define the purpose of your group.** In church circles, "small group" means different things to different people. Some groups are primarily get-to-know-each-other gatherings. Some focus on serious Bible teaching, some on a more interactive exploration of scripture. Others are accountability groups where participants should expect to get down and personal. Groups may gather people around a common interest or cause. All of these options have relational and ministry value. Clarify the purpose of your particular group so people know what to expect when they join.

**Get to know your group members.** In the vast majority of cases, people are in a small group because they want to be there. Why? Spend some time exploring what motivates the women in your group to be there. Some have deep Bible background, and others are just getting to know Jesus. Some women thrive on talking, while others like to listen. Some are ready to be friends immediately, but others need some time to feel secure. The spectrum is wide, so find out where the people in your group would put themselves, and be sensitive as you leave room for everyone to grow.

**Set the parameters.** A group of about eight to twelve is conducive to good conversation and building relationships. However, if your group's purpose is accountability, you will want a smaller, more intimate group. Once you decide when to meet, respect the schedule. Making a lot of changes in meeting dates can discourage participation because it's too unpredictable. Women are busy people, especially if they have families. Respect their time. Start when you say you plan to start, and finish when you said you would finish. When the group gets into a groove, you'll discover what level of flexibility the group can tolerate.

**Make room for all personalities.** Leaders tend to lead in the style that is most comfortable to them. Teachers tend to teach according to their own learning style. Recognize this going in, and intentionally try to make room for personalities different from your own. Be careful not to show preference to people who jump in with an answer to every question you ask or with whom you seem to click more naturally.

**Encourage participation.** Personality affects participation, especially if your group is discussion based. Some people are quick to talk while others may need some time to process before speaking. Avoid putting people on the spot in ways that make them uncomfortable, but make a point to invite participation. Changes in body language may indicate that someone is ready to speak, but a quiet person likely won't interrupt a more vocal person. As the leader, you can turn to someone and say, "I wonder what you think, Lindsay," or "Marianne, you're looking thoughtful." Another way to encourage participation from quieter group members is to ask them to read aloud a Bible passage or other material you're using.

**Be prepared.** While it's true that some people are gifted to facilitate a discussion and have the background and experience to be spontaneous, most of us need to prepare. If you're studying a book or a Bible passage, be sure to study ahead of time. If you're leading a discussion, take a few minutes to plan some questions that will prompt discussion. Your preparation will show, and seeing that the leader is putting something into the group will encourage group members to do the same.

# TIPS FOR SETTING GOALS

Whether you are setting goals for yourself, for a small group, or for a larger ministry, keep in mind these simple principles for writing goals you can achieve.

**1. Be specific about what you plan to do.** Avoid being broad and vague. For instance, rather than saying, "Have a better prayer life," say something like, "Take a ten-minute prayer walk each weekday morning." If you word your goal with a specific action, you will know whether you did what you said you would.

**2. Plan how to measure your progress.** This usually involves numbers. How many minutes? How often? Suppose your small group decides to raise money to fight human trafficking. Your goal might be, "Hold one fund-raiser event every four months for the next year." Then you can see your progress. If you want to read more of the Bible, one of the beauties of a one-year reading plan is that the progress checkups are built in every day.

**3. Make sure you know what action to take, and in what period of time.** Use verbs in your goal statements. "*Invite* three friends to attend the conference with me before the registration deadline." "*Identify* four possible Bible study guides by our meeting time next month." If you have an ambitious goal, break it down into specific action steps. When you accomplish each step, move on to the next one, and you'll be that much closer to your goal.

**4. Set goals you can actually accomplish.** In a burst of enthusiasm after a retreat you might decide you want to write in your journal for an hour every day. And then real life happens. The baby gets sick or your boss schedules you for extra hours or your mother falls and breaks her hip. Let's face it, this kind of stuff happens to all of us, and things we truly intended to do simply are not possible. That leaves us feeling like failures. Set goals that challenge you but not goals that are so unrealistic that you are certain to fail. Find the balance between something that stretches you and helps you grow but at the same time is something realistic for your life.

**5. Set time limits.** Goals don't have to last until the second coming of Christ. If you want to start a new habit—healthy eating, exercise, Bible study, reading with your child, dinner with your husband, or whatever—set a goal for a few weeks, or even a few days. If you're successful, then set a goal for a longer period of time. But if you're not successful in the short term, you have an opportunity to make adjustments and start again without beating yourself up for failing. Habits don't change overnight. Give yourself the grace of second chances.

When you write a goal, make sure it is specific, measurable, action-oriented, realistic, and timely.

# SMALL GROUP ACCOUNTABILITY QUESTIONS

Here are some sample questions you might ask each other in a small accountability group. Your group can add to or adjust these questions.

*Have I been a verbal testimony to Christ?*

*Have I spent adequate time in prayer and reading God's Word?*

*Have I seen any sexually explicit material that will damage my relationship with my husband or Christ?*

*Have I spent money recklessly? Have I demonstrated good stewardship?*

*Have I intentionally honored my husband and children?*

*Have I damaged another with my words?*

*Have I given in to an addiction in my life?*

*Have I remained angry toward another?*

*Have I wished misfortune or hardship on anyone?*

*Have I been totally honest today?*

*Have I allowed any person or circumstance to rob me of my joy?*

# RECOMMENDED READING

*Shared Blessings: Inspiration for a Woman's Heart* (Barbour Publishing, 2010).

Ninety devotional readings from Circle of Friends writers provide a spiritual boost. This compilation focuses on God's kindness and all the good things he provides.

*Bouquets: Intentional Relationships in Making Disciples* by Bruce Hamsher (Herald Press, 2008).

Choosing to develop relationships with people outside our normal circles carries the opportunity to bring people to Christ. When we cultivate relationships, we live out the scripture's call to be the fragrance of Christ.

*Boundaries: When to Say Yes, When to Say No to Take Control of Your Life* by Henry Cloud and John Townsend (Zondervan, 1992).

Learn to set reasonable boundaries that keep you on the path God lays out for you. God's purpose for you does not have to be lost amid the demands of your life.

*Experiencing God: Knowing and Doing the Will of God* by Henry Blackaby (B&H Books, revised 2008).

This modern classic features basic scriptural truths that teach us how to develop a true relationship with God and discover how God is working in and through us.

*A New Kind of Normal: Hope-Filled Choices When Life Turns Upside Down* by Carol Kent (Thomas Nelson, 2007).

The author knows what it is like to live through horrendous life-altering experiences and still choose hope, life, gratitude, forgiveness, and trust.

*Between a Rock and a Grace Place: Divine Surprises in the Tight Spots of Life* by Carol Kent (Zondervan, 2010).

When life shatters, grace still abounds. Carol Kent writes poignantly of her own experiences with sorrow and the light of God's grace that shines in dark places.

*The Great House of God* by Max Lucado (Thomas Nelson, 2001).

God does not want to be your escape from life. He wants to be where you live. Lucado uses the Lord's Prayer as a floor plan that draws God's children close.

*So Long, Insecurity* by Beth Moore (Tyndale House, 2010).

Popular Bible teacher Beth Moore exposes the realities of the insecurity many women feel at home and in the workplace and shines the light of God's truth on each one.

*Love and War: Finding the Marriage You've Dreamed Of* by John and Staci Eldredge (Doubleday, 2009).

The authors offer honest, direct advice on companionship, the mission of your marriage, sex, and realizing that Satan, rather than your spouse, is the enemy. Recognize your own brokenness and find your life in God.

*Sheet Music: Uncovering the Secrets of Sexual Intimacy in Marriage* by Kevin Leman (Tyndale House, 2003).

Sex is a gift from God to treasure and enjoy. This book helps you look at your own experience and how to enrich it for a satisfying sexual relationship.

*Have a New Kid by Friday* by Kevin Leman (Revell, 2010).

Find out why kids act the way they do, understand your own attitude as a parent, and start using simple strategies that will transform your relationship with your child of any age.

*The Birth Order Book* by Kevin Leman (Revell, revised 2009)

This is a fascinating look at how being the oldest, the youngest, or somewhere in between affects personality, relationships, parenting styles, and career. Learn more about how your birth order influences how you interact with the world and what you can do about it.

*The Purpose Driven Life: What on Earth Am I Here For?* by Rick Warren (Zondervan, 2002).

Worship, community, discipleship, ministry, and evangelism are key to a life rich in meaning. Every person has a purpose according to God's divine plan. How can you find your place in what God is doing?

*Fashioned by Faith* by Rachel Lee Carter (Thomas Nelson, 2011).

Everyone knows we live in a "skin-is-in" society, heavily driven by media and immodesty. So how does a young Christian woman reconcile a fashinable wardrobe with maintaining her integrity?

# Find *Your*
# PLACE TO BELONG

*Visit the Website,
Where You Can Find…*

+ Information on starting your own Circle of Friends
+ More about the book *A Place to Belong*
+ Book trailer and videos

# www.findaplacetobelong.com

# ABOUT THE AUTHOR

**Lisa Troyer** enjoys spending time with her husband, Bob, and their children, Jillian and Christian. Pursuing her passion for women's ministry, she serves as president of Circle of Friends Ministries, Inc., and has focused on the outreach, growth, and encouragement of women for over a decade. Since the debut of her program on Moody Radio, the expansion of the Circle of Friends' vision of "Acceptance, Authenticity, Affirmation, Accountability & Action" has steadily grown across the nation. With a passion for worship and songwriting, Lisa's recent single, "You Are My Shelter," with the Circle of Friends worship team, reached #2 on the Christian Music Weekly Worship Chart and is featured in the upcoming Zondervan DVD series based on Carol Kent's book *Between a Rock and a Grace Place*. Lisa has signed a music publishing agreement with Kingsway in London's ThankYou Music. Learn more about Lisa at www.lisatroyer.com.

# Joining Lisa for ministry events are her circle of friends. . .

**Dawn Yoder** has been married to Jeff Yoder for twenty years, and they have four children together between the ages of 7 and 18. She is the CEO of a 500+ employee company, a worship leader, and songwriter. She has recently released her first CD entitled "Love Me Back To Life." The project is a compelling musical companion to the novel published by Barbour Publishing, which was written by Missy Horsfall and Susan Stevens. In addition to being a board member of Circle of Friends, Dawn is also blessed to be a part of an organization called La Red, which seeks to bring values and principled thinking, based on the book of Proverbs, into all aspects of society—including business, government, and education. Dawn, along with Lisa Troyer and Jocelyn Hamsher, continue to speak encouragement into the lives of women within the church and in the corporate world. Dawn, Lisa, and Jocelyn are also available to do presentations via the John Maxwell Coaching Network.Learn more about Dawn at www.dawnyoder.com.

**Jocelyn Hamsher** and her husband, Bruce, live in Sugarcreek, Ohio, with their three sons, Micah, Ty, and Cade. Jocelyn has been working in women's ministry for more than a decade and currently serves as vice president of Circle of Friends Ministries, where she teaches, speaks, writes, and mentors. Not only does she enjoy writing devotionals for Circle of Friends (which can be read at www.circleoffriends.fm), but she has also enjoyed co-authoring *Meet Me at the Well*, a companionship Bible study (in association with Barbour Publishing, 2010) to Virelle Kidder's, *Meet Me at the Well* (Moody Publishing, 2008). She is also a contributing author in *Shared Blessings* and *Shared Hope*—Circle of Friends' devotionals (Barbour Publishing, 2010 and 2011). Her new book, *Do These Jeans Make Me Look Fat? Breaking the Cultural Mirror* (Barbour Publishing) will be released in January of 2012.

Jocelyn has served as the Director of Women's Ministries in her church as well as serving as a chaplain in the local justice center and retirement community. She is a board-certified biblical counselor, licensed chaplain, and public relations director at Heini's Cheese in Berlin, Ohio. To contact Jocelyn visit www.jocelynhamsher.com.

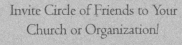